The

Twelve Steps

and

Twelve Traditions

of

Overeaters

Anonymous

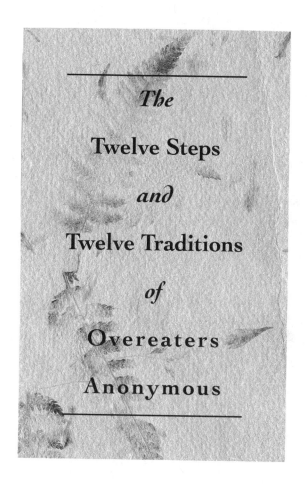

The

Twelve Steps

and

Twelve Traditions

of

Overeaters

Anonymous

ISBN 0-9609898-6-2
Library of Congress Catalog Card No.: 93-85052

Overeaters Anonymous, Inc.
World Service Office
6075 Zenith Court NE
Rio Rancho, NM 87124-6424 USA
Mail Address: P.O. Box 44020
Rio Rancho, NM 87174-4020 USA
1-505-891-2664

Overeaters Anonymous is a Fellowship of individuals who, through shared experience, strength, and hope, are recovering from compulsive overeating. We welcome everyone who wants to stop eating compulsively. There are no dues or fees for members; we are self-supporting through our own contributions, neither soliciting nor accepting outside donations. OA is not affiliated with any public or private organization, political movement, ideology, or religious doctrine; we take no position on outside issues. Our primary purpose is to abstain from compulsive overeating and to carry this message of recovery to those who still suffer.

CONTENTS

INTRODUCTION TO THE TWELVE STEPS

We of Overeaters Anonymous have found in this Fellowship a way to recover from the disease of compulsive overeating. After years of guilt over repeated failures to control our eating and our weight, we now have a solution that works. Our solution is a program of recovery—a program of twelve simple steps. By following these steps, thousands of compulsive overeaters have stopped eating compulsively.

In OA we have no program of diets and exercise, no scales, no magic pills. What we do have to offer is far greater than any of these things—a Fellowship in which we find and share the healing power of love. Our common bonds are two: the disease of compulsive eating from which we all have suffered, and the solution that we all are finding as we live by the principles embodied in these steps. Since our program is based on the twelve steps, we would like to offer here a study of those steps, sharing how we follow them to recover from compulsive eating. We hope in this way to provide help for those who still suffer from our disease.

The second half of this book contains a study of the twelve traditions of Overeaters Anonymous, showing how our individual groups and OA as a whole solve problems and continue to carry the message of recovery to compulsive overeaters.

If you think you may be a compulsive overeater, give yourself a chance for recovery by trying the OA program. Our way of life, based on these twelve steps and twelve traditions, has brought us physical, emotional, and spiritual healing that we don't hesitate to call miraculous. What works for us will work for you, too.

*We admitted we were
powerless over food — that our lives
had become unmanageable.*

In Overeaters Anonymous we begin our program of recovery by admitting that we're powerless over food. Some of us have difficulty with this admission because we've had so much experience in trying to control our eating. At one time, or periodically, most of us were able to do so. Our eating may be out of control right now, we persisted in thinking, but someday soon we'll again muster the strength of character needed to check our eating excesses, and this time we'll keep them under control. For all of us, however, the days of controlled eating grew fewer and farther apart, until at last we came to OA, looking for a new solution.

In OA we learn that a lack of willpower isn't what makes us compulsive overeaters. In fact, compulsive overeaters often exhibit an exceptional amount of willpower. But compulsive eating is an illness that cannot be controlled by willpower. None of us decided to have this disorder, any more than we would have decided to have any other disease. We can now cease blaming ourselves or others for our compulsive eating.

The disease of compulsive eating is threefold in nature: physical, emotional, and spiritual. Compulsive eating does not stem simply from bad eating habits learned in childhood, nor just from adjustment problems, nor merely from a love of food, though all three of these may be factors in its development. It may be that many of us were born with a physical or emotional predisposition to eat compulsively. Whatever the cause, today we are not like normal people when it comes to eating.

Like compulsive overeaters, normal eaters will sometimes find pleasure and escape from life's problems in excess food. Compulsive overeaters, however, often have an abnormal reaction when we overindulge. We can't quit. A normal eater gets full and loses interest in food. We compulsive overeaters crave more. Some of us even have a strange reaction to particular foods: while others can comfortably eat single portions of these foods, we feel compelled to eat another serving after we've finished the first...and then another...and another. Not all compulsive overeaters can identify particular foods which give us this trouble, but many of us can. What all of us have in common is that our bodies and minds seem to send us signals about food which are quite different from those the normal eater receives. We have found through much experience that no matter how long we abstain from eating compulsively, and no matter how adept we become at facing life's problems, we will always have these abnormal tendencies. Those of us who have returned to our former compulsive eating behaviors, even after years in recovery, have found it harder than ever to stop.

Clearly, if we are to live free of the bondage of

compulsive eating, we must abstain from all foods and eating behaviors which cause us problems. If we don't ever overeat, we won't trigger the reaction that makes us crave more. But this, too, has proven impossible for us to do by our willpower alone. Before we found OA, every diet or period of control was followed by a period of uncontrolled eating. This is because our malady was not just physical in nature; it was emotional and spiritual as well. We were obsessed with food, and no amount of self-control or weight loss could cure us. Because of this obsession, the day always came when the excess food looked so inviting to us we couldn't resist, and our firm resolutions were forgotten. Sooner or later we always started overeating again and gradually (or rapidly) the eating worsened until at last we were out of control.

This mental obsession was something we couldn't be rid of by our unaided human will. Another power, stronger than ourselves, had to be found to relieve us of it, if we were to stop eating compulsively and stay stopped.

Most of us have tried to deny to ourselves that we have this disease. In OA we are encouraged to take a good look at our compulsive eating, obesity, and the self-destructive things we have done to avoid obesity— the dieting, starving, over-exercising, or purging. Once we honestly examine our histories, we can deny it no longer: our eating and our attitudes toward food are not normal; we have this disease.

Part two of step one, admitting "that our lives had

become unmanageable," has also been difficult for many of us. We felt that we had managed very well in life, despite our problems with food and weight. Many of us held down responsible jobs and ran our households with reasonable success. We had friends who liked us, and many of us had fairly good marriages. That these didn't make us happy was surely due to the fact that we were fat (or felt we were). If we could just get to the perfect weight, life would be perfect. Surely it would be exaggerating to say we were incapable of managing our lives. We certainly could use some help with the compulsive eating, but with the rest of life, we were doing fine.

Again, an honest look at our lives helped us to take step one. Were we really excelling at our jobs, or just getting by? Were our homes pleasant places to be, or had we been living in an atmosphere of depression or anger? Had our chronic unhappiness over our eating problems affected our friendships and marriages? Were we truly in touch with our feelings, or had we buried our anger and fear in false cheerfulness?

We sometimes recognized we had living problems, but felt that life would be manageable if only we could stop the compulsive eating. Whenever we did stop, however, we found life without excess food unbearable. Even getting to our desired weight didn't cure our unhappiness.

Many of us believed that our lives would be manageable if only others around us would do as we wanted. We thought everything would be fine if only our bosses would recognize our worth, if only our spouses would give us the attention we needed, if only our children were well-behaved, if only our parents would leave us alone. Our lives became unmanageable when the car wouldn't start, the computer broke down, or our checking account wouldn't balance. We suffered from other people's unmanaged lives or from bad luck. What alternative did we have? We ate to sate the fears, the anxieties, the angers, the disappointments. We ate to escape the pressures of our problems or the boredom of everyday life. We procrastinated, we hid, and we ate.

Before we came to OA and began discussing our experiences honestly with other compulsive overeaters, we didn't realize how much we had damaged ourselves and others by attempting to manage every detail of life. It was only after we began to recover that we saw the childish self-centeredness of our willful actions. By trying to control others through manipulation and direct force, we had hurt our loved ones. When we tried to control ourselves, we wound up demoralized. Even when we succeeded, it wasn't enough to make us happy. We hid from our pain by eating, so we didn't learn from our mistakes; we never grew up.

Some of us resisted step one because it seemed like negative thinking. If we tell ourselves we're powerless over food, we reasoned, then we program ourselves to go right on eating compulsively!

Later we discovered that, far from being a negative factor, the admission of our powerlessness over food opened the door to an amazing newfound power. For the first time in our lives, we recognized, acknowledged, and accepted the truth about ourselves. We *are* compulsive overeaters. We *do* have an incurable disease. Diabetics who need to be on insulin risk blindness and possible death unless they recognize the truth of their diabetic condition, accept it, and take the prescribed medication. So it is with compulsive overeaters. As long as we refuse to recognize that we have this debilitating and ultimately fatal disease, we are not motivated to get the daily treatment for it which brings about our recovery. Denial of the truth leads to destruction. Only an honest admission to ourselves of the reality of our condition can save us from our destructive eating.

The same principle applies to our unmanageable lives. As long as we believe that we already know what is best for us, we cling to our habitual ways of thinking and acting. Yet these ways of thinking and acting got us into the unhealthy, unhappy condition we were in when we came to OA. In step one, we acknowledge this truth about ourselves: our current methods of managing have not been successful, and we need to find a new approach to life. Having acknowledged this truth, we are free to change and to learn.

Once we have become teachable, we can give up old thought and behavior patterns which have failed us in the past, beginning with our attempts to control our eating and our weight. Honest appraisal of our experience has convinced us that we can't handle life through self-will alone. First we grasp this knowledge intellectually, and then finally we come to believe it in our hearts. When this happens, we have taken the first step and are ready to move ahead in our program of recovery.

Came to believe that a Power greater than ourselves could restore us to sanity.

Many of us compulsive overeaters tend to look at this step and say: "Restore me to sanity? I don't need that. I'm perfectly sane. I just have an eating problem." But how sane are we, really?

When we look with complete honesty at our lives, we see that where eating is concerned we have acted in an extremely irrational and self-destructive manner. Under the compulsion to overeat, many of us have done things no sane person would think of doing. We have driven miles in the dead of night to satisfy a craving for food. We have eaten food that was frozen, burnt, stale, or even dangerously spoiled. We have eaten food off of other people's plates, off the floor, off the ground. We have dug food out of the garbage and eaten it.

We have frequently lied about what we have eaten —lied to others because we didn't want to face the truth ourselves. We have stolen food from our friends, family, and employers, as well as from the grocery store. We have also stolen money to buy food. We have eaten beyond the point of being full, beyond the point of being sick of eating. We have continued to overeat, knowing all the while we were disfiguring and maiming our bodies. We have isolated ourselves to eat, damaging our relationships and denying ourselves a full social life. For the sake of our compulsive eating, we have turned ourselves into objects of ridicule and we have destroyed our health.

Then, horrified by what we were doing to ourselves with food, we became obsessed with diets. We spent hundreds of dollars on weight-loss schemes, we bought all sorts of appetite-control drugs, we joined diet clubs and spas, we had ourselves hypnotized and analyzed, we had major surgery on our digestive systems, we had our ears stapled or our jaws wired shut. All of this we did willingly, hoping we could someday "have our cake and eat it too."

Some of us went from doctor to doctor looking for a cure. The doctors gave us diets, but we had no better success with those than with the other diets we'd been on. The doctors gave us shots and pills. Those worked for a while, but we inevitably lost control and overate again, putting back on the weight we had worked so hard to lose.

Many of us tried fasting, with and without a doctor's supervision. Usually we lost weight, but as soon as we started eating again, the compulsive eating behavior returned, along with the weight. Some of us learned to purge ourselves with vomiting, laxatives, or excessive exercise. We'd stuff food in our mouths until we were in physical pain, then we'd "get rid of it." We damaged our digestive systems and our teeth while we starved our bodies of nutrients needed to live.

Those of us who were overweight got plenty of advice

from others about how to get to our "ideal" size, but nothing permanently solved our problem. We found that no matter what we did to ease our turmoil, our compulsive eating eventually returned. Over the long haul, our weight went up and our self-esteem went down. After a while we became battle-weary and discouraged. Still we could never accept our powerlessness. The prospect of being obese, sick, and out of control for the rest of our lives led some of us to conclude that life was simply not worth living. Many of us thought about suicide. Some of us tried it.

Most of us, however, never reached suicidal desperation. Instead we took comfort in a feeling that everything was all right as long as we got enough to eat. The only trouble was that as our compulsive eating progressed it became harder for us to get enough. Instead of bringing comfort, the overeating backfired. The more we ate the more we suffered, yet we continued to overeat. Our true insanity could be seen in the fact that we kept right on trying to find comfort in excess food, long after it began to cause us misery.

Once we honestly looked at our lives, it became easy for us to admit we had acted insanely where food and weight were concerned. Many of us, however, were able to confine our compulsive eating to the hours when we were alone and to carry on with relatively normal lives. We worked hard during the day and ate hard at night. Surely we were sane in most respects.

More self-examination revealed many areas in which our lives were out of balance. We had to admit that we had not acted sanely when we responded to our children's needs for attention by yelling at them, or when we were jealously possessive of our mates. Too much of the time we had lived in fear and anxiety. More comfortable with food than with people, we sometimes limited our social lives. We drew the drapes, disconnected the telephone, and hid in the house.

When we were around other people, we smiled and agreed when we really wanted to say no. Some of us were unable to stand up for ourselves in abusive relationships; we felt we deserved the abuse. Or we focused on others' faults and thought for hours about what they should do to solve their problems, while our own problems went unsolved.

Compulsive overeaters are often people of extremes. We overreacted to slight provocations while ignoring the real issues in our lives. We were obsessively busy, then we were "wiped out" and unable to act. We were wildly excited then deeply depressed. We saw the whole world in black and white. If we couldn't have it all, we didn't want any; if we couldn't be the best, we didn't want to play the game.

Little by little, we saw how much pain our way of living was causing us. Gradually, we came to believe we needed to change. In all of life, as well as with the food, we were irrational, unbalanced, insane. If our willpower and determination couldn't change our unsuccessful way of living, what could? Clearly a Power greater than ourselves had to be found if we were to be restored to sanity.

At this point most of us had trouble for one reason or another with step two. Some of us did not believe in God. We despaired of finding a solution to our problems if that meant we had to "find God." Some of us walked out of our first meeting when we heard that three-letter word mentioned and didn't return until years more of compulsive eating had made us desperate. Those of us who stuck around made a wonderful discovery. OA doesn't tell us we have to believe in God—only that a Power greater than ourselves could restore us to sanity. We are invited to define that Power however we wish and relate to it in whatever way works for us. OA only suggests that we remain open to spiritual growth and show tolerance for others by neither criticizing nor promoting specific religious doctrines in OA meetings.

Ours is a spiritual program, not a religious one. We have no creeds or doctrines, only our own experiences of recovery. Atheists and agnostics are welcome in OA and have found recovery.

How have we who were not believers in God come to believe in a Higher Power?

It usually started as we sat in an OA meeting and experienced the camaraderie of our fellow compulsive overeaters. Here were people who understood us and cared about us. We could be totally honest about ourselves and they still accepted us unconditionally. This acceptance grew into love, carrying with it a power that seemed to stay with us as we left our OA meetings. It was not too great a leap of faith to believe that this shared love was a Power greater than ourselves that could lead us to sanity. The love of the group, then, became our Higher Power.

Before long we usually asked other OA members to be our sponsors. Most of us chose someone with whom we felt a kinship or in whom we saw recovery. As we developed personal relationships with our sponsors, the love of the OA group came to us in a deeper way. They answered our questions, listened to our problems, shared our tears and laughter, and guided us in recovery as they helped us apply OA principles in our lives. For the first time ever we felt the relief of not having to face our problems alone. This relationship was a Higher Power in which we could believe.

However, OAs are human. Sometimes, when our groups or sponsors failed us in some way, we felt cut off from the support which had come to mean so much to us and our new sanity seemed threatened. We now needed a more reliable way of relating to a Higher Power. At this point we learned we could "act as if." This didn't mean we were to be dishonestly pious or pretend we believed in God when we didn't. It meant we were free to set aside theological arguments and examine the idea of spiritual power in light of our own desperate need for help with our lives.

Some of us began by asking ourselves: "What do I need from a Higher Power? What would I like such a Power to be and to do in my life?" Once we identified this Power for ourselves, we found we felt at ease with it. Then we began to act as if such a Power existed and we found good things happening to us as a result. Little by little, as we experienced changes for the better in our lives, we came to believe in a Power greater than ourselves which could restore us to sanity.

Those of us who arrived at OA with a set of religious beliefs usually looked at this step and said, "No problem. I'm beyond that step. I already believe in God." Then, to our dismay, some of us found ourselves having more trouble with the OA program than the agnostic or atheist. Sometimes we religious ones had trouble because we believed in God's existence, but we didn't really believe God could and would deal with our compulsive eating. Perhaps we didn't believe that our compulsive eating was a spiritual problem, or we felt that God was concerned only with more important matters and expected us to control such a simple thing as our eating. We failed to understand that God loves us in our totality and is willing and able to help us in everything we do, that God will help us with every decision, even food choices and amounts.

Many of us had asked God to help us control our weight and this prayer hadn't worked. Later we understood why our pleas for help seemed to fall on deaf ears. What we were really asking God to do was remove our fat while allowing us to go on eating whatever we wanted, whenever we wanted. Most of us also needed to learn to ask other people for help and let God speak to us through our fellows. In OA, God's healing power comes to us through a caring community of other compulsive overeaters. Before we joined the OA Fellowship our prayers for help might have gone unanswered simply because we were never meant to face this disease in isolation. We were meant to open up so that we might learn to truly love others.

Whatever the case, after years of making vows and saying prayers but then eating compulsively again, we were left without faith that God could restore us to sanity about food. We believed intellectually that God could do anything, but deep in our hearts we "knew" God couldn't help us with this area of our lives. It was this negative concept about God we had to change if we were to find recovery. How could we do this? We became willing to start fresh with our Higher Power. Our heartfelt concept of God wasn't working, so we became willing for it to be changed. Just like the atheist or agnostic, we could begin to do this by asking ourselves what, exactly, we needed and wanted God to be to us and to do for us. Then we acted as if God were really exactly what we wanted and needed our Higher Power to be. We became willing to let go of any concept about God which wasn't helping us to recover from compulsive eating. We had to replace our old ideas about God with a faith that worked. This was both humbling and frightening for us, but once we became willing to do it, surprising things began to happen.

For all of us—atheists, agnostics, and religious ones alike—coming to believe was something that happened as we began taking actions which others told us had worked for them. Whether or not we believed these actions would work for us didn't seem to matter. Once we took the action and saw it work, we began to believe. Then we tried other suggestions and our lives began to be transformed.

This willingness to act on faith, then, was the key to step two. It was the beginning of a healing process that would relieve us of the compulsion to overeat and bring stability to our unbalanced lives. As we responded with action to the love we had been shown in OA, the result was a new faith in ourselves, in others, and in the power of that love. We had begun to develop a new relationship with a Power greater than ourselves, and we were ready to move ahead with our program of recovery.

Made a decision to turn our will and our lives over to the care of God as we understood Him.

It has been said that the first three steps of the Overeaters Anonymous program are simply: "I can't; God can; I think I'll let God!" In step one we became convinced that we could manage neither our eating nor our other living problems by our own will alone. In step two we added to this acceptance of our utter helplessness a newfound faith that there exists a Power greater than us which can relieve us of the obsession for food and restore us to sanity in all areas of life.

It is impossible to take step three until we have taken the first two steps. Once we have fully acknowledged our fatal powerlessness and have come to believe that there is a solution, however, the third step is simple. If we want to live free of the killing disease of compulsive eating, we accept help without reservation from a Power greater than ourselves. We now say yes to this Power, deciding from here on to follow spiritual guidance in making every decision.

Note we have said this step is simple; we have not said it is easy. It is not easy, because for every one of us this decision means we must now adopt a new and unfamiliar way of thinking and acting on life. From now on, we let go of our preconceived notions about what is right for us. When faced with choices, we earnestly seek guidance from our Higher Power, and when that guidance comes we act on it.

Our new way of life begins with a willingness to adopt a whole new attitude about weight control, body image, and eating. Our twelve-step program is the most important way OA differs from the diet and weight-loss programs we tried in the past. Those systems gave us diets to follow but made *us* responsible for adhering to them. In OA we are given no diets. Weight loss is not our only goal, and we accept that even a "perfect" body (if there were such a thing) would not make us happy. Our primary purpose is to abstain from eating compulsively, and we know that in order to do so we will need help.

At one time or another since we joined OA, most of us have experienced a period of complete freedom from the obsession with food and the compulsion to overeat. For many of us, this freedom came when we took step three and turned the entire problem over to our Higher Power. Suddenly we no longer thought much about food and eating. When mealtime came, we ate moderately, felt satisfied, and stopped eating. It was as if some miracle had given us a healthy attitude about food and eating.

For most of us, however, this reprieve didn't last forever. Gradually food regained its dominance in our thoughts. Eventually the day came when we again wanted food we didn't need, and staying away from eating compulsively became more difficult for us. Did

this mean that we really hadn't taken step three after all? Sometimes that was the case, but usually it simply meant the OA honeymoon was over. What we needed now was a way of being abstinent over the long haul and living sanely through good times and bad.

Often we caused ourselves problems because we didn't realize that there were some kinds of eating we could handle comfortably and some kinds we couldn't. Many OAs have been able to identify certain eating behaviors or foods which tend to lead us into compulsive eating. Acceptance of these facts about ourselves gives us hope, for we know that by simply eliminating these eating behaviors and foods from our lives we will experience fewer struggles with our disease. In OA, however, there's no list of foods and measurements or dos and don'ts which defines abstinence. We are individuals with our own individual nutritional needs, and we've found that what is a healthy choice for some of us might be lethal for others. People who come to OA are sometimes confused by the lack of dietary regulations. "If OA doesn't give us any rules to follow," they ask, "how are we to find the guidance we must have to avoid compulsive eating?" The decision we have made in step three answers this important question. We have found that when we give up self-will regarding food and completely turn our lives over to our Higher Power, we receive all kinds of guidance.

For instance, after years spent in the struggle with this disease, some of us have been able to take an honest look at our past experience and identify for ourselves the specific kinds of eating that give us the most trouble. Others of us have been given eating restrictions by qualified professionals because of special physical problems or needs. Many of us know much about sound nutrition, but we have never before been able to put this knowledge into effect because our food obsession interfered. Now that we are working the steps, we have been given the power of choice about our eating. Our common sense will tell us to avoid our own particular problem areas and follow sound nutritional guidelines.

At times when we have felt confused about abstinence, many of us have been helped by discussing our particular problems with our sponsors. Of course the final responsibility for what we eat and don't eat rests with us, but we have found that a sponsor can often make suggestions which help us find our way.

All of this experience, knowledge, and help is augmented by a source of wisdom inside us that becomes more powerful as we recover from compulsive eating and develop our relationship with our Higher Power through prayer and meditation. This inner resource is our intuition. When we place our will and our lives in God's care in step three, we give God our intuition as well. Intuition is supposed to be God's direct line into our minds and hearts, but our problems and our self-will have interfered with this connection. As we work the steps, the interference begins to be removed, and intuition begins to function properly, helping us focus on God's will, both for our eating and for the living of our lives.

It is important to bear in mind that knowledge about ourselves and our nutritional needs is useless without the kind of help we find in OA, because we remain powerless to apply it. Many of us have tried for years to find the perfect way of eating and stick to it. In order to continue being abstinent, we will have to have a Power greater than ourselves operating daily in our lives. This is always available to us as long as we continue working the twelve steps and living out our decision to trust God's guidance in everything we do. As we become aware of what our eating guidelines should be, we ask God for the willingness and the ability to live within them each day. We ask and we receive, first the willingness, and then the ability. We can count on this without fail.

As we continue abstaining, we find we can depend upon God to eliminate our yearning for the kind of eating that harms us. Much of the time, we no longer want to eat unwisely and we come to prefer foods that are good for us. This miracle of sanity is an everyday reality for thousands of recovering compulsive overeaters. We find we are seldom obsessed with eating and food, so that it is possible for us to continue eating moderate, nutritious meals, one day at a time, day after day, month after month, year after year.

Do we ever achieve a permanent freedom from food obsession? Yes and no. OA veterans do have this miraculous freedom most days, but occasionally the obsession returns. How do we get through these times without overeating? We don't panic. Instead we quietly reaffirm our personal guidelines and ask our Higher Power to help us continue living within them. Then we turn away from food and eating to focus our attention on our OA Fellowship and the twelve steps. As we work the steps, using the tools of the program—abstinence, literature, writing, meetings, the telephone, sponsorship, anonymity, and service—we find the help we need. OA friends lovingly remind us that "this too shall pass." It does pass, and our obsession is lifted again. This abstinent way of life continues on a daily basis so long as we continue to trust a Higher Power with our lives, renewing our step-three commitment daily.

Inexperienced in this way of living, many of us have asked, "How do I reach this decision to turn my will and life over to a Higher Power? What exactly do I have to do?" It helps to understand that once we make this decision, our approach to all choices will be like our approach to our food and eating choices. We will no longer simply do what we feel like doing or what we think we can get away with. Instead, we will earnestly seek to learn God's will for us, then we will act accordingly. We give up fear and indecision, knowing that if we are sincere, our Higher Power will give us the knowledge of our best course in life, along with the willingness and ability to follow that course, even when it seems difficult and uncomfortable.

In learning God's will, we may again refer to our experience, knowledge, common sense, intuition, and the wisdom of spiritual mentors. If something has repeatedly worked well for us or for someone else in a similar situation, we may assume it will work in our present situation, ultimately bringing good to us and to others, which is God's will. For instance, we might find from experience that when we're feeling unstable, going to OA meetings usually restores our sanity. Thus, we can assume it's God's will for us to keep attending meetings regularly, even when we don't feel like it. Or, when we're in a group of people who are gossiping about someone we dislike, we might be inclined at first to join in with a few comments of our own. But we've learned from experience that gossip is not good for us, so we know it's God's will that we not take part in the damaging conversation. We need no burning bush and ethereal voice to tell us what God wants for us in most of our choices each day. Honesty, common sense, and a sincere willingness to follow our new spiritual path are sufficient to show us the way.

When we face indecision we remember the words of the Big Book, *Alcoholics Anonymous:* "Here we ask God for inspiration, an intuitive thought or a decision. We relax and take it easy. We don't struggle. We are often surprised how the right answers come after we have tried this for a while. What used to be the hunch or the occasional inspiration gradually becomes a working part of the mind."[1]

In making major decisions, of course, we will not assume that every thought which comes into our minds

1. Reprinted from *Alcoholics Anonymous,* 3rd ed. (New York: Alcoholics Anonymous World Services, Inc., 1976), pp. 86-87, by permission of the publisher.

is inspired by God. When we're considering taking an unusual action we will want to consult with a sponsor or spiritual guide. It is not this person's job to decide for us; no human can do that. But a person who is detached from our immediate situation and has some experience in this way of life can help us apply sound spiritual principles in learning our Higher Power's will for us.

This, then, is how we will operate our lives, once we have made the decision called for in step three. None of us can follow this way of life perfectly, but we find that our success in recovery and our freedom from food obsession are in direct proportion to how sincerely we try to live in this manner.

What it takes to work step three is a real willingness to live by God's will, one day at a time. Having this willingness, we do not let any doubt or confusion we may still have keep us from acting. We concentrate on wherever or whatever we think God might be, and we say out loud, in words of our own choosing, that we now turn our will and our lives over to our Higher Power, holding nothing back.

When we say this prayer and mean it, we have made the key, life-changing decision which will lead us to recovery. We have taken the third step. We now have a new reaction when we face a problem or a decision, whether it has to do with food, with life, or with our own runaway emotions. Instead of acting on impulse, we pause long enough to learn God's will. Then, instead of resorting to willpower, we relax and reach out to receive help from our Higher Power. All we need say is, "God, please help me do your will."

Once we compulsive overeaters truly take the third step, we cannot fail to recover. As we live out our decision day by day, our Higher Power guides us through the remaining nine steps. When we falter, we are reminded of our commitment to live by God's will alone, and we trust that the willingness and ability will come if we only ask for them. When we get off track, our Higher Power will guide us back, as long as we are sincerely trying to know and do God's will. We can confidently face any situation life brings, because we no longer have to face it alone. We have what we need any time we are willing to let go of self-will and humbly ask for help.

*Made a searching and fearless
moral inventory of ourselves.*

The fourth step calls for us to examine our lives up to the present day, writing down all important actions and events of a moral or ethical nature, our feelings about them, and the character traits in us from which these actions stemmed. Writing this inventory is an important process which tests our commitment to the twelve-step program. How can we face this challenge fearlessly, as the step asks us to do?

Those of us who have completed step four have found that taking this searching and fearless moral inventory was one of the most loving things we ever did for ourselves. As we took an honest look at the past, at who we'd been and what we'd done, we began to understand ourselves better. That understanding was the beginning of emotional healing. Many of us had lived our lives up to this point with a secret feeling of shame. We carried deep in our hearts the feeling that we were worthless or insignificant. Often this shame stemmed from unresolved guilt over mistakes we'd never fully dealt with. We had never faced our wrongs honestly and acknowledged them, so we were left feeling ashamed. Writing our step-four inventory enabled us to begin cleaning up the messes of the past so we could start life over, afresh.

The self-analysis we do in step four is essential to our recovery from compulsive eating. This step continues a process of transformation which began with our admission of powerlessness in step one, a process of increasing honesty and self-awareness that will gradually free us from our bondage to self. Our past problems have been controlling our actions and feelings for years, often in ways of which we are not aware. As we face the problems, they lose their power to overwhelm and control us. The chains of self-obsession drop from us one by one, and we are able to know and do our Higher Power's will more easily, without the need to protect ourselves from uncomfortable feelings by eating compulsively.

We find it best to approach this inventory with the words "fearless" and "searching" uppermost in our minds. Many of us have become experts in self-deception after years of lying to ourselves about how much we were eating and the problems our compulsive eating was causing us physically, emotionally, and spiritually. We've lied to ourselves about our other problems, too, denying that we've made mistakes, that we've been wrong about things, that we need to change. We *must* change if we are to recover. Change begins with honesty. As we work the fourth step, we develop a new ability to see our own dishonesty and a greater willingness to live by truth.

Ideally, step four is an inventory to be taken after

we have stopped eating compulsively, so that we will have the clarity of mind to be thorough in our self-examination. Some of us, however, have gone ahead with the fourth-step inventory as soon as we finished the first three steps, even though we weren't yet abstinent. We found that writing the inventory helped us live by our decision in step three, and in many cases helped us become abstinent.

In fact, we've learned that delaying the fourth step until we feel we can do it "perfectly" only delays our recovery. Some of us spent months seeking advice from sponsors, friends, and people at meetings, studying all sorts of literature on the subject, looking for the one "right" way to do step four. When our sponsors told us, "the important thing is just to *do* it," we didn't understand. We didn't realize until after we took the step that perfectionism was one of the troublesome defects of character we needed to get rid of.

Many of us delayed beginning step four simply because we didn't want to do it. We said we were not yet willing, but when it came right down to it, being *willing* to do the inventory and *wanting* to do it were two different things. Sometimes we began the program with enthusiasm but fell back into the disease while waiting for the desire to do step four to overtake us. We have found that a simple prayer for willingness works to get us going on the inventory, especially when the prayer is followed by some further action. Any action, no matter how small, will help us to overcome deadly procrastination. It helps, too, if we will follow through with a commitment to work on the step regularly and faithfully until it is completed.

We found it was necessary to write our inventories. Anyone who has taken an inventory in a store or other business will verify that it is difficult to keep track of what we have in stock unless we write it down. The writing process helped us to examine the feelings that went with our actions. We began to see clearly how some of our reactions had served us well while others had unbalanced us emotionally, setting up patterns of negative thinking and self-destructive behavior.

Sometimes we began step four without knowing why it was necessary, doing it simply because we had been told it would help us recover from compulsive eating. We tried it and it worked. This is one example of what we mean when we say that in OA we learn to utilize, not analyze. Those of us who tried to analyze the step and why it might work soon found we were wasting time. Nor did it help to analyze ourselves before we did the step. It worked far better when we plunged in and started writing.

What form should our inventory take? Any form at all, since we are writing for ourselves and are never required to show our inventories to anyone. In fact, we find that *how* we do the fourth-step inventory makes little difference. What counts is that we do it. Our sponsors can help by suggesting ways to approach our inventories, and they serve as invaluable sounding boards during the writing process.

Many of us have used the guidelines set forth in the

Big Book, *Alcoholics Anonymous*, pages 64-71,[1] and have found this to be an excellent way to take inventory. We begin by writing down names of people, institutions, and principles toward which we feel resentment, fear, or other uncomfortable feelings. Then, beside each name we write down events which have caused us to have those feelings. Finally, beside each event we write down the basic instinct in us which was affected by the incident and any defective character traits in us which might have placed us in a position to be hurt.

It is easier for most of us to proceed with step four if we take time to acknowledge our assets in addition to our shortcomings. No matter how many problems we have, each of us also has positive characteristics; it's important that we recognize them at some point during the inventory process. There are various approaches to this. Some OAs find it helpful to list personal assets and accomplishments at the very beginning of the inventory. Some of us run a line down the middle of each page, then list positive characteristics, details, and examples from our personal histories on one side, and negative characteristics, details, and examples on the other side. Others devote a paragraph to each asset followed by another paragraph about the corresponding liability. Some of us have done our inventories in chronological form, listing

---

1. *Alcoholics Anonymous,* 3rd ed. (New York: Alcoholics Anonymous World Services, Inc., 1976).

events, emotions, and positive and negative characteristics by periods of time. Taking such a balanced view
of ourselves encourages us to be more objective, and
helps us to doggedly search out our defects without
fear.

One good way to inventory ourselves is to ask ourselves questions about specific character traits. Then
we examine in writing the ways that we've exhibited
these characteristics in our lives.

For instance, we might ask ourselves if we have
been prideful. Have arrogance and false pride characterized our behavior? If so, we list them in our inventory. Then, we illustrate the characteristic of pride by
listing examples of how pride has caused us to act.

> *Are we power hungry? Do we enjoy controlling
> others? In what ways have we tried to control our
> spouses, parents, brothers or sisters, children,
> friends, employers, colleagues, teachers, or oth-
> ers? Do we manipulate people? Do we intimidate
> them?*
>
> *Have we been jealously possessive of a mate or
> friend?*
>
> *How do we react when we don't get our own way?*
>
> *How do we react when people disagree with us?*
>
> *Are we intolerant of differences?*
>
> *Do we try to smooth stormy waters, or are we
> troublemakers?*

Have we insisted on being the center of attention? Have we acted offensively just to be noticed? Are we afraid that we won't be recognized or respected or loved? Do we fear that we won't get our share or that we won't be listened to? Do we push to be first in line? How has prideful self-centeredness caused us to act?

Are we status-seekers? How much money, time, and energy have we spent trying to impress or show ourselves better than others?

Are we snobs? Do we pay more attention to "VIPs" than to "ordinary" people?

Have we sought to put people down or put them in their place?

Have we repeatedly belittled anyone?

Have we ever played a mean trick on anyone?

Have we condemned others for things we're also guilty of? Are we hypocrites, even as we denounce the hypocrisy of others?

Have we ever deliberately defamed someone?

Do we indulge in gossip ourselves or listen to and enjoy the gossip of others?

Are we oversensitive, quick to take offense at what people say to us? Or do we laugh everything off, pretending nothing hurts us?

Are we selfish, letting our own desires govern us

while we ignore the needs of others? Have we spent money our families needed in order to feed our illness or gratify our other desires? Have we been unavailable to our children or our mates when they needed us?

Or do we let the needs of others govern us while we ignore our own? Do we take on other people's responsibilities, doing for them the things they should be doing for themselves?

Are we willing to claim responsibility for the problems we've caused, or have we tried to shift the blame to others? When have we rationalized our misbehavior?

Are we bigoted? Have we ever denied anyone fair treatment because of race, religion, politics, gender, or disability? Do we tell ethnic, racist, or sexist jokes? If not, are we afraid to say that we don't enjoy such "humor"?

Can we admit our mistakes and acknowledge that others are sometimes right? Are we teachable or complacent?

Do we accept our own failings and those of others as natural, or do we criticize, condemn, and complain?

Are we people-pleasers? Do we need everybody to like us, so much so that we make it our goal to find out what people want and give it to them, no

*matter the cost to ourselves? Are we afraid to say
no to others?*

*Are we defiant, either openly or secretly? What is
our attitude toward laws, rules, and people who
have legitimate authority over us?*

As we take inventory we also look at our fears. For
many of us, fear, worry, and anxiety have played a key
role in our lives, robbing us of joy and keeping us from
fulfilling our dreams. It is not until we take inventory
in step four that we begin to realize that we don't have
to live with fear. First we list the people, places, and
things that have caused us fear. Then we look at other
ways fear has affected us.

*Are we anxious about the future? How much of
our time do we spend worrying?*

*Are we afraid of people? Do we isolate ourselves
from our friends or society?*

*Are we afraid to reach out to new people? Have
we held back from others, waiting for them to
come to us?*

*Do we repeatedly get into relationships with the
kind of people who mentally or physically abuse us?*

*Are we afraid to end existing relationships which
are destructive or inappropriate for us?*

*Have we delayed seeking new jobs or careers,
held back by worry and fear? Are we so afraid of
change that we remain in situations that are not
good for us?*

Are we afraid to express ourselves, to tell others how we feel?

Are we so afraid of conflict that we accept abuse rather than risk asserting ourselves?

When has fear held us back from taking other actions we should have pursued? Have we stood by and allowed another person to be hurt when we could have done something to prevent it? Did we ever let another person get blamed or punished for something we did?

Have we ever abandoned a person we had a responsibility to help?

Anger and resentment are common manifestations of our disease. In fact, most of us ate compulsively when we felt anger or resentment. As we continue writing our inventories, it is important to list the people and institutions we've held grudges against.

Are we holding onto a grudge because at one time or another someone threatened or damaged our self-esteem, security, ambitions, or relationships? Have we tried to get even with people who hurt us? Do we make a point of never forgetting when someone does us harm?

Do we hold a grudge against anyone due to jealousy? Are we envious of other people's appearance, wealth, sex life, popularity, possessions, or position in society? If so, we list these jealousies in our inventory.

Do we carry grudges against ourselves for things we did or failed to do, or for the fact that we're compulsive overeaters? If so, we include ourselves on our grudge list.

Looking at our anger, we ask ourselves whether we tend to be harsh, unforgiving, and self-righteous.

Do we misdirect our anger? Do we lash out at those closest to us, rather than telling the person at whom we're really annoyed why we're angry?

Have we abused others verbally or physically? We need to list each incident we can remember in which we struck out at another person.

Have we ever abused animals?

Have we ever taken anyone's life because of our anger, fear, carelessness, or another reason?

How has greed affected our lives? Are we generous or selfish? Are we satisfied when our needs are filled, or are we always wanting more, seldom content with what we have?

Are we obsessed with money? Do we believe more money would solve all our problems? Do we spend money faster than we can make it? Are we responsible managers of the money we have? Do we pay our bills?

In what ways have we been lazy and slothful? Have we been procrastinators? If so, we write it down, along with incidents in which we have pro-

crastinated. Are we perfectionists? Do we delay starting things we are afraid we can't do to perfection?

Or, on the other hand, do we carelessly rush into things without due thought? Are we impatient?

Do we do our share of the work in groups we're a part of, or do we sit back and wait for someone else to volunteer?

Are we overly dependent on others? Do we expect them to protect us from the consequences of our actions, to make us feel good, or to take care of things we should be doing for ourselves?

How about lust? What problems has sex caused us?

Have we pursued sex in ways that damaged our self-esteem? Have we been promiscuous?

Have we spent hours fantasizing about sex when we might have been building better relationships?

Have we been interested only in our own pleasure, never seeking to please our sexual partner as well?

Have we ever sought to satisfy our sexual impulses at the expense of others?

Have we slept with another person's spouse or lover? Have we cheated on our own spouse or lover?

Have we ever forced or manipulated anyone to have sexual contact with us?

Have we ever sexually molested anyone? Have we ever had sexual contact with a child or with anyone who was not fully capable of resisting?

Have we ever abused a position of trust to get sex from someone who sought our help?

Have we used intimidation to get sex? Have we abused a position of power? Have we ever threatened or sought revenge against someone who wouldn't go along with our sexual advances?

Have we used sex or pregnancy to trap someone in a relationship?

Have we ever gotten someone pregnant and not shared responsibility for it?

Have we transmitted a disease when we knew we were infected?

In what other ways have we misused our sexual drives? Compulsive eating has made many of us uninterested in sex. Have we been unfair to our partners and ourselves, preferring isolation and food to the risk of physical intimacy?

Do we trust people, or do we have faith in no one, including ourselves?

Perhaps we have not been able to trust because we haven't been trustworthy. A willingness to be honest is essential to recovery in OA. How often do we tell the truth? How much do we lie? To whom have we lied and under what circumstances? What have we lied about?

Have we been sneaky or practiced deception? Have we taken advantage of someone's ignorance instead of telling the full truth?

Have we kept money or items we found instead of returning them to their rightful owners?

Have we ever stolen anything?

We need to list each incident we can remember in which we have taken money, food, or other things which didn't belong to us.

Did we ever damage anyone's property and not repair or pay for the damage?

Have we ever cheated anyone out of money or possessions? In what cases have we borrowed things and not returned them?

Have we ever broken a confidence?

Have we ever cheated on tests or in games or contests? Do we make a habit of cheating?

Have we cheated and lied to ourselves? Have we lived in denial about our eating, our character defects, or our need to change?

Negative thinking is another form of self-deception which plagues many compulsive overeaters. Do we tend to dwell on the dark side of things?

Are we thankful for what we have, or do we ignore our blessings and focus on what we lack?

Are we optimistic or pessimistic? Do we concentrate on working for good, or do we become obsessed with bad things which might happen to us?

Has our negative outlook made life bleak for others who live and work with us? Have we been cynical and critical?

Have we indulged in self-pity? Have we played the martyr?

Negative thinking, like fear, is a habit many of us have had to let go of as we have recovered.

After writing our inventory, we review it. Have we listed everything we can think of about ourselves, constructive as well as destructive? We've found that we need to write down all our characteristics, tendencies, feelings, prejudices, and the actions we have taken as a result. Some of our actions will be painful for us to recall, but we write them down anyway. When we face the guilt that truthfully tells us, "You made a mistake," we're freed of shame that falsely tells us, "You *are* a mistake."

Once we've made the inventory, checked it and reviewed it, we ask God to help us remember anything more that belongs there. We spend some time in quiet meditation, concentrating on our complete willingness to face whatever truths about ourselves God wants to show us. If we realize we have left out an important item, we add it to our inventory. As we continue toward recovery we'll find more shortcomings, and more positive characteristics. Right now, however, all we need to do is list everything we are aware of at present. Having done this as honestly as we can, we trust that we have written a searching and fearless moral inventory of ourselves. We have completed step four.

Looking back over what we have written, we shouldn't be discouraged if the negative outweighs the positive. After all, if we found nothing wrong, we wouldn't need our program of recovery. In fact, we've found that the more defects we uncover, the more our lives can improve as we continue working the twelve steps.

Each of us who completes a fourth-step inventory in OA finds it essential to our recovery and a major factor in changing our lives. As we reach the end of step four, we discover that a promise made in *Overeaters Anonymous*'s "Our Invitation To You" has begun to be fulfilled. We are "moving beyond the food and the emotional havoc to a fuller living experience."[2]

2. *Overeaters Anonymous* (Overeaters Anonymous, Inc., 1980), p. 3.

Admitted to God, to ourselves, and to another human being the exact nature of our wrongs.

Throughout our lives many of us have felt isolated from other people. We felt that we were outsiders, and we acted out this feeling in many ways, some of us by being shy, others by being arrogant or belligerent, others by playing the clown. No matter how we acted, however, deep down we felt alone and apart. Now, looking at the fifth step, we see something we can do—a positive action which we can take—to end our isolation.

By the time we reach this point in our OA program, most of us are already feeling less alone. Since joining Overeaters Anonymous we've learned to accept the loving welcome we've found and to be part of a Fellowship. We've talked with others over the phone, shared at meetings, and discussed our lives in depth with our sponsors. We've begun to make true friends in OA, friends with whom we can speak honestly. Perhaps it has become easy to share about how we, too, acted while we were eating compulsively. On a deeper level, however, we probably realize that there is still much of ourselves we haven't shared. This is natural. Few of us had ever done a moral inventory before we joined OA, and our fourth-step inventory brought us new insights and understandings.

By the time we have completed the fourth step, most of us feel ready to move ahead quickly with step five. We want to be free of resentments, guilt, and shame rooted in the past, and we realize that sharing the details of our past with another human being is an important step toward freedom. Once we have taken this step, we will no longer have anything to hide. This is the beginning of the end of our isolation.

Step five starts with our Higher Power. Most of us find that without the help of a Power greater than ourselves we are incapable of complete honesty about the mistakes we have made. It is human nature to cling to the illusion that we have done no wrong, and through years of compulsive eating we have become experts at rationalization. Now, with God's help, we leave rationalization behind and begin to practice integrity. We face the reality of our mistakes. We see the part we ourselves have played in creating our own misfortunes, and we realize the futility of continuing to blame others for our compulsive eating and our unmanageable lives.

In step five we are learning a new way of life. From now on, we will readily acknowledge our wrongs instead of seeking to hide them from ourselves and others. A humble admission of our mistakes to God is our first step in this new direction. We willingly open our hearts so that a life-changing power can come in and heal us. We go back over our fourth-step inventory, acknowledging each truth about our past behavior, no matter how painful or embarrassing. In acknowledging these wrongs to God, we begin at last to acknowledge them to ourselves, too. We admit to ourselves who we are and what we've done. As we do this, we gain new hope. We start to feel that we can be forgiven and begin life anew with a clean slate.

Once we have made the admissions to God and to ourselves, we may feel we have fully dealt with our past. What need is there, we may ask, to air our "dirty laundry" in front of another person? Won't this self-revelation simply humiliate us and further lower our already low self-esteem?

In practice, step five has the opposite effect. When we actually do our fifth step with another human being, we find that we are humbled without being humiliated. Many of us have always felt that we had to be better than everybody else or we were no good at all. Through the fifth-step process, we begin to see reality. All our striving to get ahead has been useless. We are neither above nor below the rest of the human race; we're a part of it, shaped by the same basic needs and desires as all our fellows. Those of us who have belittled ourselves or felt we were worse than others also gain a new perspective. In talking honestly with another person about ourselves, we begin to feel a sense of relief. Someone knows all about us and still accepts us unconditionally. We begin to forgive ourselves and see ourselves as capable, strong, and honest. And so we are: in taking step five we prove ourselves capable of accomplishing a difficult task and strong enough to be completely honest with another human being.

Indeed, admitting the exact nature of our wrongs to

another human being has been a frightening prospect for most of us, for we've never before risked such complete openness with another person. Yet, we find that we haven't truly admitted our wrongs to ourselves until we speak about them with someone else. It is only through the process of discussing our shortcomings out loud with an understanding person that we can finally begin to know ourselves and accept ourselves. Nothing in us can be changed until we first accept it. Step five, by helping us to know and accept ourselves, makes it possible for us to change and recover.

It is important that we choose a trustworthy and understanding person with whom to complete step five. For many of us that person is the sponsor who helped us take the first four steps of the program. Others of us have found that we feel more comfortable confiding in a person other than our sponsor. Either way is the "right" way, so long as it is right for us. We understand that if we pick a person other than our sponsor, we are not rejecting our sponsor.

Any person who is recovering in a twelve-step fellowship and who has completed the fifth step herself or himself is usually a good choice to listen to our fifth step. Such a person will easily understand what we are trying to accomplish with step five. However, there is no rule which says we cannot give our fifth step to someone outside the program—a therapist, for instance, or a religious counselor. We ask for God's guidance, we give the matter some thought, then we move ahead.

We are not looking for someone to tell us how to manage our problems. What we need is a loving witness, someone who will keep our confidences and will listen without judging us or seeking to fix us. Also, we want to confide in someone who'll be objective enough to tell us if there's something glaring we've omitted and who can guide us through this process if needed. Step five is usually our first attempt to fully open our hearts to another human being. Most of us need loving guidance in learning this new skill.

When working this step we do more than just recite events from the past which we consider to be our wrongs. We need to discuss the "exact nature" of those wrongs. This means we will need to talk about *why* we did the things we did. What feelings led to our actions and what did we feel afterward? We need to look at what those actions cost us. For instance, it's not enough to acknowledge that we have held a grudge against a certain person; we also need to talk about what it is in our nature that causes us to react that way. Are we jealous? Have we been resentful because of our thwarted desire to control another person? Then we discuss how these negative feelings and actions have affected us materially, emotionally, and spiritually.

Sometimes coming to understand our motives helps us to forgive ourselves. Often we see that, at some level, we were fighting for survival when we did the things we did. Most of us find that fear is at the root of many of our damaging emotions and actions. As we grow in the twelve-step way of life, we learn that our fears usually stem from our inability to trust that our basic needs will be met. Perhaps we have good reasons for our mistrust; perhaps people have failed us, placing us in situations we were not emotionally prepared to handle. Still, we find we have to outgrow our doubts. If we are to recover, we must learn to trust other people and entrust our lives to a Power greater than ourselves.

For all of us, learning this kind of trust has been a gradual process, taking a long time. Our fifth step is a giant stride forward in this process. By opening our past life to another human being and showing this witness our deepest secrets, we are making ourselves vulnerable in a way we have not been since childhood.

Can we trust that this person won't use this knowledge to hurt us? Determined to get well, we willingly take the risk. When we do, a miracle happens. Another human being knows us truly and fully, yet accepts us anyway. We begin to experience trust, and we feel that if another person can accept us unconditionally, perhaps we can accept ourselves unconditionally as well.

Sometimes the process of doing steps four and five brings to our awareness more than our character defects. Sometimes we uncover old traumas: experiences of being abandoned, abused, sexually molested, or raped, are far more common among us than anybody would like to believe. These and other memories have been so deeply painful to those of us who were victims that we have spent our lives running from them and eating to cover them up. Until we began to deal with them, some of us found that our abstinence was precarious or we continued to feel unhappy, even while we were abstaining and working the steps. In such cases, some of us have supplemented our OA program with therapy from qualified professionals and groups especially geared to helping us deal with these issues. At the same time, most of us find that therapy alone doesn't permanently solve our eating problems. We need a continued involvement with the twelve steps and OA for continued abstinence and recovery.

As we complete step five, we may feel many emotions, among them humility, elation, and relief. We often feel nearer than ever before to our Higher Power and more loving and trusting of other people. Whether we feel these things or not, we can rest assured that we *are* nearer to God and more capable of trusting others. The fruits of having faithfully completed step five may be apparent immediately or gradually, but they will appear. Having taken step five, we are free at last. The great burden of our past mistakes has been lifted from us. We find we can face each day and each challenge as it comes.

In the process of sharing our inventory we have become more honest with ourselves and others than we have ever been before. Honesty is a key factor in our recovery from compulsive eating, and so we will want to develop this trait. The best way to do so is to continue working the twelve steps. In this way we can learn how to deal with those troubling aspects of ourselves which we discovered in steps four and five. Simply knowing what is wrong with us isn't always enough. Steps six through twelve will show us more actions we can take to bring about the necessary changes in our lives. From this point on, we begin to leave behind the character defects which have caused us so many problems in the past.

*Were entirely ready to have God
remove all these defects of character.*

At first glance step six seems easy. After all, who among us would not want to have all our problems miraculously removed, once we have identified them? As soon as possible we want to get on with the business of being perfect people. Many of us are tempted to pass quickly over the sixth step without giving it due thought.

"Go ahead, God!" we say. "I'm entirely ready." Then we swear off the old self-destructive behaviors, only to find ourselves right back in their grip within a short time. "I *know* better than this!" we berate ourselves. Our character defects seem to stick to us like glue as we try time and again to turn them over to God.

In practice, step six turns out to be one of the most difficult of the twelve steps, because *saying* we're entirely ready and *being* entirely ready are two very different things. What we are entirely ready for, actually, is to have the difficulties our defects cause us removed while we hang on to the defects themselves.

Why is it so hard for us to be entirely ready to part with our defects? One major reason for most of us is fear. We are comfortable with our old ways of thinking and acting, even though we know they are harmful. We have no idea what we'd do without them because we've never known how to cope with life any other way. Often we feel we'd be less interesting as human beings without some of our defects. While we don't enjoy the pain they often cause us, they are so much a part of us that the thought of having them suddenly removed is threatening to us. Perhaps resentments have dominated our thinking for so long that we don't know what else to think about. Or maybe we're afraid that if God eliminates our cynicism, lying, and gossiping, we'll be left with nothing interesting to talk about. We admit that our old ways of relating to other people have caused pain and we want to let go of them. But how *will* we act? In honestly facing step six, we confront the fear that our defects are like threads woven into the very fabric of our being; if God removes them we feel we'll surely come unraveled.

Often we face an even more difficult obstacle. Some of our defects are not only familiar and comfortable to us, they're also enjoyable. We get a rush of excitement from telling a lie and getting away with it, so we say to ourselves our falsehoods, after all, are harmless "white" lies. Our fantasies make us feel important, so we overlook how they waste the time we could be using to deal with our real lives. We enjoy picking up juicy tidbits of gossip and passing them on, so we rationalize that the people we're talking about deserve it, or that they'll never find out. Some of us get a charge out of having a fight or throwing a temper tantrum and the control over other people that these outbursts have usually gained us. Say what we will about being "completely ready" in a general way to have God remove our shortcomings, when it comes to specifics, we'd rather hang on to a few of the choice ones.

For these reasons we're tempted to rationalize the sixth step itself. "After all, nobody expects us to be perfect," we say. "We strive for progress, not perfection." Such reasoning only delays our recovery. The sixth step calls for us to be *entirely* ready to have God remove *all* our defects of character. Those of us who take this step with the total commitment required to make it work do indeed strive for the ultimate refinement of our character.

Even when we do approach it with complete willingness, another problem often arises with step six. Some of us misunderstand this step and act as if it's up to us to remove our own shortcomings. In our attempts to be rid of dishonesty, for instance, we may try to reform and become honest. Or we see we've been selfish, so we try to be generous. Anger is one of our problems, so we try never to get angry. Or we've heard that fear is incompatible with faith, so we try not to feel any fear.

All these are good efforts, but they often seem to get us nowhere. The harder we try to rid ourselves of our defects, the more they control us. Because we have misread step six, we are totally defeated in our attempts to work it. Thus we learn a key truth about ourselves and our twelve-step program. We are powerless over each of our defects of character, just as we are powerless over the food. It will be up to a Power greater than ourselves to remove them from us; we can't do it alone.

Does this mean we shouldn't try to change our behavior until our Higher Power changes us? Should we continue being dishonest, intolerant, and all the rest? Of course not. Being "entirely ready" means that we firmly turn our backs on the old self-destructive behaviors and make every effort to act and live by the principles embodied in the twelve steps. But we shouldn't become discouraged if we find that we aren't changing as quickly as we would like. We can't expect to be free of all our defects overnight. What we are asked to do in step six is to become entirely ready for this miracle of release to happen to us, no matter what it may cost us, no matter what in our lives may change.

When we work step six, we dedicate ourselves to a lifetime of growth and change. Being entirely ready means that we are completely willing to recognize and let go of our defective behavior patterns, and to let God change us as God will. We don't set the timetable or method for these changes. When and how our defects are removed is entirely up to God. Our work is to do what we can to make ourselves ready, by actively reaching for recovery and putting ourselves in the frame of mind to receive God's help.

We might begin to do this by submitting each defect to close scrutiny. In steps four and five we took a long hard look at each trait and acknowledged it as a part of our lives. Now we ask ourselves what it is doing *for* us as well as what it is doing *to* us. We search out our reasons for hanging on to each trait. Perhaps one has been a readily available source of comfort, while another has added excitement to our lives and a third has enabled us to compensate for our lack of self-esteem. Every character defect we have today has been useful to us at some point in our lives, and we need to recognize that fact.

Next, we need to recognize that each of these old tools for coping with life has now outlived its usefulness. We look at the harm it is doing us to cling to each of these ways of thinking and acting. As we had to "hit bottom" regarding our eating behavior, so we now need to hit bottom with each of these traits. Only when we fully realize that they are costing us more than they are giving us do we become entirely ready to be rid of our defects of character.

Working the sixth step is a lot like working the first three steps with each of our defects. We remind ourselves: "I'm powerless to rid myself of this trait. I can't, but God can, and I'll let God take it."

A willingness to change is the essence of step six. Change is always frightening, even when it's a much-needed and long-overdue change for the better. Many of us have wasted years and suffered a lot of pain in order to avoid having to change. As we face step six, we recognize and acknowledge our human fear of change. Then, because we are willing to go to any length for recovery from compulsive eating, we move ahead with this step anyhow. No longer will we allow fear to keep us from doing what is best for us. After all, we have confronted the first five steps, taken them in spite of our fear, and lived to tell the story. By the time we reach step six, we're almost used to doing the very things we've been the most afraid of.

As with the five earlier steps, our rewards when we've taken step six are great. Although we may not realize it at first, our commitment to embrace the needed changes in ourselves has given us an extraordinary power to deal with life's challenges. No longer do we go through life clinging desperately to the past, resistant to change. From now on, we will strive to keep ourselves entirely ready for any transformations our Higher Power wants to bring about in us. Having such an attitude, we cannot fail. We will become wiser, saner, more effective people as we recover from the disease of compulsive eating. We'll find we can cope with both good times—and bad, learning and growing spiritually from each experience, as our Higher Power intended us to do all along.

Humbly asked Him to remove
our shortcomings.

Having become completely ready to let go of our defects of character in step six, we find that step seven is simple; all we have to do is say a prayer, requesting that God take our shortcomings from us. There is a qualification, however. As we say the prayer, step seven calls for us to adopt an attitude of humility.

Many of us misunderstood the concept of humility at first; we confused it with humiliation or low self-esteem. We felt we had suffered enough humiliation to last a lifetime, and we balked when our fellow OAs suggested we might need to become more humble. Humility was not what we needed, we felt; low self-esteem was a big part of our problem! In OA we learned that low self-esteem was not at all the same as humility. In fact, a poor self-image keeps us in bondage to self and thus makes it impossible for us to find true humility.

As we began to recover in OA, we could see how compulsive eating had caused us to be obsessed with ourselves and our status. Humiliated by our inability to control our intake of food and by the devastating consequences of compulsive eating, we fought for self-esteem with all our might. As our disease progressed and our compulsive eating worsened, our self-esteem fell progressively lower, and we fought ever harder to bolster it by gaining whatever mastery we could over our fellow beings. In our self-absorption, we became status-seekers in one way or another. Primarily concerned with getting our own way and the recognition we craved, we tried openly or secretly to place ourselves above other people, hoping to disprove our own feelings of inadequacy.

In OA we have discovered that humility is simply an awareness of who we really are today and a willingness to become all that we can be. Genuine humility brings an end to the feelings of inadequacy, the self-absorption, and the status-seeking. Humility, as we encounter it in our OA Fellowship, places us neither above nor below other people on some imagined ladder of worth. It places us exactly where we belong, on an equal footing with our fellow beings and in harmony with God.

If we have earnestly worked the first six steps of the program, we have already come a long way toward this new attitude of humility. We have admitted our need for help to live our lives, have begun to let go of self-will, have become willing to acknowledge our true selves—defects and all—and have become willing to have our self-defeating attitudes and traits changed. Before we can ask for these changes with genuine humility, however, there are several concepts which it will be helpful for us to understand.

First, we are not asking God to remove our shortcomings so that we can be better than other people. This kind of self-righteousness would be a step backward in our journey to recovery. Self-righteousness moti-vates us when we find ourselves looking down on others who are not working the twelve steps, whether they are people outside OA or newcomers to our Fellowship. As we take step seven, our goal is not to make ourselves more moral than others. It is simply to draw closer to being the people God intends us to be. We pray to be made new, not for our own gratifica-tion, but so that we may be more useful instruments of our Higher Power.

Second, it often happens that a shortcoming isn't removed immediately, or it returns after being gone for a while. Every one of us has experienced struggles with some of our character defects, even after praying for their removal. The existence of the struggle is not a sign that we lack humility. But what attitude do we take during those difficult times? If we are surprised, shocked, deflated, or discouraged when a defect returns, we lack humility. If we get angry at God, our-selves, or other people because we have the defect, we lack humility. Real humility about our character defects carries with it *acceptance*. We accept that each defect, as painful to us as it may be, is a part of who we are. With humble acceptance we can quietly say to our Higher Power, "I am this way, and only with your help can I change."

On the other side of the coin, humility means that we aren't smug when a defect which has long been a part of our lives is removed; we're genuinely relieved. We recognize our release from the defect as a miracle, evidence of the power of God's healing love, and we are honestly grateful. Instead of approaching those who still suffer a similar problem with an attitude of superiority, we offer them hope. They may well say to themselves, "If she (or he) can change, surely I can too!"

Obviously, this kind of humility is not something we can lay hold of simply by willing ourselves to be humble. Humility is a gift as surely as is our recovery from compulsive eating and the other miracles of healing we experience as we work the twelve steps. Our job is to be willing to let go of old attitudes which block humility, such as low self-esteem, status-seeking, and self-righteousness.

Our approach to step seven, then, might begin with a prayer for genuine humility. Having said this prayer, we can proceed with the rest of step seven, trusting that our Higher Power will grant us the gift of humility to a greater and greater degree, one day at a time, as we continue to let go of our old values and practice the principles of the twelve steps. We don't have to wait until we achieve perfect humility to proceed with step seven and the remaining five steps. (We might be waiting a long time.) We proceed with our step-seven prayer, secure in the knowledge that we have done our part and God will do the rest.

How do we complete step seven? Quite simply, we take our written inventory or list of character defects in hand. (Some of us have found it helpful to assume a physical posture of humility as we pray.) With our list before us, we name each shortcoming individually and ask God to deal with it whenever and however God wants. We express our complete willingness to have each shortcoming removed from us. We express our desire to become more effective in serving and helping others as our shortcomings are transformed into assets. Having said this prayer, we have taken step seven.

Can we now expect to miraculously become perfect beings? Perhaps not. In fact, as we continue with the twelve steps, we will almost certainly discover defects we didn't see during the housecleaning we undertook in steps four through seven. Humility means that we will no longer be shocked and horrified when we realize we have yet another defect. We begin with the premise that there could be many things about us which need to change, only some of which we're able to see at any given time. In God's time, when God knows we're ready, we will be given new insights into our true defects of character—we will, that is, if we are honestly working our program. When this happens, we apply the principles of the program, including those of steps six and seven. We fully acknowledge and accept the shortcoming as belonging to us. We then examine our motives and the effect this problem is having on our lives until we are sure we're ready to let go of it. We acknowledge our powerlessness to remove the defect ourselves and humbly ask God to take it from us; then we get up and go on with life in a new frame of mind, knowing that God will indeed remove the shortcoming.

Often we will be shown actions which we are to take as each defect is being removed. For instance, we may visualize ourselves as the people we will be when we no longer have each particular defect. How will we think and act? We may find it helpful to rehearse what we'll say and do when tempted to act in the old self-destructive ways. Sometimes we'll be caught off guard and fall back into the defective patterns, but if we persist in visualizing and practicing better ways of life, they will, with our Higher Power's help, eventually become second nature. When we make a mistake, we acknowledge that fact without claiming that we ourselves *are* that mistake. From now on, we cease telling ourselves we are always going to be dishonest, selfish, abusive, stupid, or bad people. Instead, we repeatedly affirm to ourselves the truth about ourselves—that we are becoming honest, caring, nurturing, wise, and effective human beings as we practice our new behaviors, day by day.

These actions may seem like hard work at first, but we've found that our willingness to act is an important factor in our healing. It indicates our sincerity. Are we willing to make an investment of time and energy to change our attitudes and actions? To what lengths are we willing to go in order to be rid of these shortcomings? Effort on our part will help us to appreciate the miracle we are about to receive, rather than take it for granted. Yet when the miracle happens, we know for certain that we didn't simply "clean up our act." We took action under the guidance of our Higher Power, and God worked through us to remove our shortcomings.

In order to live sanely and grow spiritually as we continue to refrain from compulsive eating one day at a time, we find it best to make the principles we have learned in steps six and seven a part of our daily lives. We cultivate the willingness to have any newly discovered fears, resentments, and other shortcomings removed. Then, as part of our daily prayer and meditation, we hold these defects up to the light of God's love and humbly ask God to remove them from us, being willing to take any action our Higher Power would have us take.

If we are patient and persistent, we will learn much about ourselves and why we feel and act the way we do. We might see that some of our shortcomings are simply misapplied character traits. When applied to the right things at the right times, these same traits which have hurt us so much become great assets. For example, stubbornness is a shortcoming when it keeps us from letting go of self-destructive behaviors. When working a twelve-step program, however, stubbornness can be an asset. It may be the only thing that keeps us coming back, practicing the principles, and using the tools of the program, even when we're slow to see results. In order to "remove" a shortcoming such as stubbornness, our Higher Power might help us to understand it as perseverance and to use it correctly.

Repeated practice of step seven enables us to form a working partnership with our Higher Power through which we are relieved of the defects which have blocked our effectiveness in the world. As we gain new humility and ever greater freedom from our character defects, God's power flows more surely and freely through us, bringing healing to others as well as ourselves, and drawing to us all the things we once fought so hard to attain: self-esteem, a feeling of usefulness, joy, strength to surmount difficulties, fellowship, and love. Our simple prayers, humbly spoken, are answered in wonderful ways as we open our lives to God's transforming power, and we find that God does for us what we could never do for ourselves.

*Made a list of all persons
we had harmed and became willing
to make amends to them all.*

In our days of out-of-control eating, most of us were so obsessed with food we had little time to develop or nurture effective relationships with other people. When we were eating compulsively, we may not have fully realized how we had isolated ourselves. We may have felt that once the food problem was solved, everything in our lives would be satisfactory. When we did stop eating compulsively, however, we usually found that our defective ways of dealing with others were a source of pain for us. In many cases, this pain was so great we were tempted to eat again rather than face it. "What's the use of abstaining if I'm just going to hurt?" we asked. "If this is recovery, I don't want it!"

Clearly, if we were going to remain abstinent and find serenity, we had to learn better ways of dealing with other people, ways that would bring us joy instead of pain. Step eight is designed to help us with this process. In step eight, we look at our relationships for the purpose of discovering those patterns which have done harm to us and to others. Here we meet guilt head-on and get rid of it. Here we learn about the healing power of forgiveness as we discover how to forgive ourselves and others. Most important, we begin here to become willing to make *amends*—that is, to make *changes*—in the way we deal with the people who share our lives.

Step eight is a two-part process, the first part of which is to make a list in writing of all persons we have harmed. In deciding what names are to appear on the list, we may have some trouble sorting out what actually is harm to another person. Oddly enough, the question of how to identify harm rarely arises when we're remembering the harm done to us. We know very well what actions by others have caused *us* harm! Perhaps to help us answer the question of "what is harm" we might think about some of the ways in which we've been hurt and ask ourselves, "Have I ever dealt with another person in a similar way?" When we answer this question honestly, we may be surprised to learn that we ourselves have given others the same sort of treatment which hurt us the most when we were on the receiving end.

The written moral inventory we did in step four will help us to make a list of the people we have harmed. If our fourth-step inventory was thorough, it will probably contain information about most of the harm we are consciously aware of having done to others. As we work step eight, we look back over what we wrote on our fourth step and we draw from that inventory a list of names, adding to this list any other persons to whom we feel we owe amends. If we have lost or destroyed our fourth-step inventory, the questions in the chapter of this book about the fourth step can be used in making our eighth-step list. We go over these questions carefully, paying special attention to those which deal with ways in which our character defects have affected other people.

Many of us have found that our own name belongs somewhere near the top of our eighth-step list. Yes, we harmed other people, but we have also damaged ourselves with our self-destructive thinking, eating, and living habits. We have learned that a complete willingness to make amends to ourselves and to forgive ourselves for past mistakes has been essential to our recovery.

We will need to include the name of everyone we can remember having harmed, even those who hurt us first. It doesn't matter how badly some of these people may have treated us; we now look with complete honesty at our side of each relationship. If we did those individuals any harm at all, we need to list them and the harm we did. It might help us to remember that our purpose in doing step eight is not to judge others, but to learn attitudes of mercy and forgiveness.

On the other side of the coin, we might mistakenly go to the other extreme and put on the list names which don't belong there. If someone hurt us or was rude to us and we feel badly toward that person, we certainly need to do ourselves the favor of forgiving. However, that individual's name does not need to appear on our amends list unless we have also harmed him or her in some way. We're not doing step eight to make other people feel better or like us better, we're doing it for ourselves, so that *we* can recover from compulsive eating. In cases about which we're confused, our sponsors can help us sort out whom we have and have not harmed.

Once we have gone back through our lives in memory and are sure that we have written down the name of every person we have harmed, we are ready to grapple with the second half of step eight. Now our task is more difficult. Now we must become willing to make amends to each person on our list. In many cases this will seem like a frightening and humiliating prospect. We know we have done wrong and we are sorry for it, but to actually confess our deeds to the very people we've wronged seems impossible. After years of running from any kind of unpleasantness and hiding ourselves in food so we wouldn't have to feel embarrassment or pain, we're now asked to admit our failures and face all their consequences. And we're asked to do so while being abstinent, without eating compulsively to numb our feelings. How can we possibly become willing?

Our sponsors and other OAs who have walked this way before us will have good suggestions to help us with this task of becoming willing. At this stage of the program more than at any other, we will not want to try to go it alone. Here we will want to take our amends list to our sponsor and discuss the various problems with her or him. First of all, an experienced OA will be able to help us by making sure we actually do owe amends in each case. Further, a sponsor's suggestions about how to go about making amends will help us to become willing. As we frankly discuss the actions we might take and words we might say, the making of amends begins to seem less threatening. For the first time, we begin to feel that we really may be able to face the people we have harmed.

A sponsor will often encourage us to think about forgiveness as we work through step eight. As long as we have not forgiven people for harms they have done us, we will find it impossible to make sincere amends to them for our side of the conflicts. Even in cases where we manage to muster the willingness to talk to them, we're very likely to bring up their mistakes and wind up insulting them, rather than making amends. Even if we don't bring up their mistakes directly, our ill will toward them will come through in other ways, if we have not truly forgiven them.

Since forgiveness is obviously essential to completing step eight, some discussion of how to forgive another person is in order. Many of us have been told all our lives that we ought to forgive those who wrong us, but rarely have we been taught how to do so.

Our first step toward forgiving someone, oddly enough, might be to write down in black and white the reasons why we are angry with this person. The writing process can be very healing because more than any other tool of our program, it gets us in touch with our true feelings. Writing clarifies emotions which have been confused and buried in us, sometimes for many years. Also, by setting down our grievances in black and white, we place a boundary around them. Whether the telling of them takes up two paragraphs or twenty pages, whether it takes us minutes or hours, we finally see that there is a limit to how much we have been hurt. Our grievances are only so big and no bigger. The hurt had a beginning, and it can have an end as well.

Often, after writing out our feelings, we will find it helpful to give away what we've written in some way. Perhaps we will want to read it to a sponsor or other person not involved in the hurtful situation. Perhaps we will want to put it away for a week or so, then get it out and read it again ourselves. Often when we do this, we find that we are already feeling better about the situation, that our pain is not as great as when we first wrote it down. Finally, we may want to symbolically release the hurt, perhaps by burning the writing or tearing it up and throwing the pieces away.

If we still have bad feelings toward the person who has done us harm, we might try another powerful technique for ridding ourselves of resentments: prayer. People with long experience in living by the twelve steps have found that prayer can bring the ability to forgive even the most devastating wrongs. If we will pray for the people who have wronged us, pray for them daily, asking God to bless them with all the good things we want for ourselves, we can be freed of our resentments and unforgiveness. The action of praying for those we resent will work even if we don't mean a word of what we're saying. If we keep praying for them faithfully, sooner or later our feelings will change. When our feelings change, when we find ourselves being sincere in asking God to bless

our former enemies, then we will know we have forgiven them.

Having forgiven wrongs done to us, we find the
greatest obstacle to our willingness to make amends
has been removed. This does not mean we will suddenly want to go through with this ego-puncturing
process. In few cases will we be eager to face the people we've harmed and frankly discuss our mistakes
with them. We need to remember, however, that we
can be *willing* to do something we don't *want* to do.

As much as we might like to, we cannot skip the
making of amends. The experience of OAs who have
worked the steps before us shows that recovery depends
on completing steps eight and nine. With this in mind,
we turn once more to God, asking for the willingness
to do the things we fear, to make the amends we owe.
Having said this prayer sincerely, we are now willing,
and we move quickly ahead to step nine.

Made direct amends to such people wherever possible, except when to do so would injure them or others.

For many members of Overeaters Anonymous, step nine proves to be the most surprising of the twelve. Before we do the step, most of us dread the thought of going to each person we've harmed, frankly acknowledging our faults, and taking direct action to remedy the damage we did or repay the losses we caused. After making amends, however, those of us who dreaded step nine the most are eager to sing its praises. This step has freed us from the shackles of our past mistakes in a miraculous way. Our lives are changed, our broken relationships mended, and the ill will which poisoned our hearts for years is washed away.

Those of us still facing step nine may have heard about the benefits of making amends from those who've already done this step. Even so, our fears may make us want to procrastinate. We're warned that to put off making our amends would immobilize us and threaten our recovery from compulsive eating. As soon as we have become willing in step eight, we need to move ahead quickly and act on that willingness.

On the other hand, we also need to exercise some common sense as we set about this process. The ninth step specifically warns us of the danger of doing more harm than good as we face people directly and talk with them about hurtful situations of the past. For this reason, many of us have found it advisable to discuss the actions we are about to take with a sponsor or other person who understands the twelve-step way of life. We have probably already discussed some of our plans in the process of becoming willing to make amends. Now we need to resolve any lingering questions and doubts as to how we should proceed by checking out our words and actions ahead of time with someone more experienced than we are, someone who is detached from the situation.

Our sponsors will probably remind us that the purpose of step nine is to clear away guilt and ill will so that we may establish better relationships with people whom our lives have touched. In most cases, this will require us to do more than just say "I'm sorry." In making amends, we'll need to acknowledge the specific harm we've done, apologize, make appropriate restitution, and change our behavior toward them in the future.

Before starting out to make amends, we must let go of any expectations we may have of how the other people will receive us. In most cases we'll be treated better than we've anticipated. Sometimes people won't even remember that we ever harmed them. Others might refuse our attempts to make restitution. In some rare instances there will be those who refuse to accept our apologies. If this happens, we release these people without rancor. We cannot control how others receive our amends. They have the right to hold grudges against us the rest of their lives if they choose to. They don't owe us forgiveness, and we don't need it to complete step nine and recover from compulsive eating. Our only job is to clear off our side of the street by doing whatever we can to right our wrongs. Having done so, we no longer need to feel any guilt or anger about these situations.

Clearing off our side of the street requires us to be sincere and direct in our approach to the people we've hurt. We may be tempted to spare ourselves embarrassment by making some vague statement about being sorry for any harm we may have done. In a few cases, this is the most appropriate way in which to make amends. Most of the time, however, a loosely worded apology will not show true sincerity on our part. We need to remember that we owe the victims of our wrong actions an honest and straightforward acknowledgment of our mistakes.

At the same time, we would usually do well to keep the wording of our apologies as simple as possible, in order to avoid dragging in facts and details which might hurt people all over again. Certainly we should avoid mention of things they may have done to provoke us, even if we feel those things are much worse than our own mistakes. Having forgiven these people in step eight, we now stick to a simply worded statement of the things *we* did to cause *them* harm, and we express our sincere regrets. We avoid excuses, dramatizations, or detailed rehashing of events surrounding our actions.

We might say something like this: "Mrs. Jones, I stole money from your drawer several times when I was working for you last summer. I'm very sorry for my dishonesty." Or: "John, I realize that I made a habit of belittling you and I want to apologize. It was wrong of me to treat you that way."

In most cases we would do well to go ahead and tell the persons to whom we're making the amends what sorts of changes or restitution we are undertaking, making clear we are glad for a chance to set right our wrongs. If we have physically or materially harmed anyone, if we have stolen or damaged property, or if we have cost anyone money by our actions, we should pay or make arrangements to pay the money we owe. If we have lied to someone or about someone, we should now set the record straight, providing we can do so without causing further harm.

To amend something means to change it. We complete our amends for our wrongful actions of the past by changing our actions in the future. This is especially important when making amends to ourselves and those people close to us whom we repeatedly harmed by our patterns of behavior. We owe such people "living amends." The words we say to them will not be nearly so important as how we act toward them from now on. Were we to apologize, but then go right on hurting them, our words would be empty indeed, and a real improvement in our damaged relationships would be unlikely. Only by permanently changing our harmful attitudes and actions can we make it up to ourselves and our loved ones for the hurts of the past.

These, then, are the actions we take to make direct amends in each case where it is possible. However, there will be some people on our amends list whom we cannot find. Although direct amends to such people are impossible right now, we can begin by making indirect amends to them. For instance, we may put in writing the words we would say to them if we could see them face-to-face. We might write down our acknowledgment of the wrong we did and outline our plans to make things right with them. As we go on with our program, we'll need to continue searching for them, resolving to make the amends directly once we've found them. We are sometimes surprised by the sudden reappearance of people on our amends list who have been out of our lives for years.

Some of the people on our eighth-step list may have died, so we cannot make direct amends to them. We've found it is healing for us to go ahead and make these amends indirectly. Again, we could begin by writing down the words we would say to them if they were alive. Then we might read the letter out loud at some place that reminds us of them. The restitution part of our amends might be made by a gift to their favorite charity, by help given to a member of their family, or in some other appropriate manner.

Appropriateness should be our guide each time we make amends, whether we make them directly or indirectly. Some amends will fall in the category of those which we cannot make directly without harming somebody. For instance, to go to the spouse of someone with whom we've had an affair and confess could be very harmful, unless we're sure this person already knows about the affair. It will also help us to remember that we make direct amends for our *actions* (or inaction when action was called for) rather than for our *feelings*. To go to someone and say "I'm sorry I've disliked you all these years," is inappropriate and will only inflict pain. The appropriate way to make up for five years of secret jealousy or hatred is to replace it with five years of open acceptance, respect, and love.

Some amends may need to be made anonymously to avoid hurting innocent people. However, we don't make our amends anonymously simply to avoid embarrassment to ourselves, nor do we rationalize that making amends would injure *us* financially or damage *our* self-esteem. Were we to skip doing some of our amends, we would deprive ourselves of the full healing that comes when we work the ninth step thoroughly, and so we'd be hurting ourselves rather than doing ourselves a favor.

If we are to be restored to right relations with others, we must do whatever we can to square things with the people we have harmed. Much of what we need to do in order to make amends won't be easy, but those who have gone through with step nine have always found it to be more than worth the effort. When we finish our amends most of us feel closer to our Higher Power than ever before. As we have dealt lovingly with every person in our lives, our spiritual awakening has become a reality. To the best of our ability, we've cleaned up the wreckage of the past, and we are at peace with the world.

Now that we have completed the first nine steps, we can face the future with a new confidence. We no longer need the crutch of excess food because we have discovered a way of life which nourishes us physically, emotionally, and spiritually. Our challenge from here on will be to continue following this path as we are guided by the last three steps of our twelve-step program.

*Continued to take personal
inventory and when we were wrong,
promptly admitted it.*

Many of us have come to Overeaters Anonymous after
years of pursuing short-term solutions to our long-
term problem of compulsive eating. One aspect of this
program that keeps us here is the promise of permanent recovery from this baffling malady. But what in
this world is truly permanent? We read on page 204 of
our *For Today* book, "Repetition is the only form of
permanence that nature can achieve."[1] If we are to
experience permanent recovery from compulsive eating, we will have to repeat, day after day, the actions
that have already brought us so much healing.

Through the first nine steps of our program, we have
made a beginning on an entirely new way of life, one
that is leading us out of the mire of compulsive eating
onto the solid ground of sane eating and successful living. Though primarily intended to help us clear up the
accumulated debris of the past, action on these nine
steps has also laid down patterns for us to follow in the
future—patterns which will enable us to thrive, grow
spiritually, and be happy without excess food. Step ten
calls for daily repetition of these actions, following the

1. *For Today* (Overeaters Anonymous, Inc., 1982), p. 204.

new patterns, so that we may experience recovery every day.

The tenth step begins with the word "continued," our first clue that perseverance is about to become a key aspect of our recovery program. In the past, we may have clung stubbornly to self-destructive eating and other harmful behaviors. Now we will need to be stubborn about working our program, even during those times when we feel as though it isn't working or we aren't recovering quickly enough. Stubbornness turned to such good use becomes perseverance as we continue—day after day—to apply to our lives the same concepts we learned in steps four through nine.

In step four, for instance, we learned to take a personal moral inventory, to look honestly and fearlessly at ourselves, and to recognize our assets and liabilities. Step ten asks us to continue this practice daily. The purpose of step ten is to identify and remove from our path today's stumbling blocks, those manifestations of pride, fear, anger, self-pity, greed, and other emotions which are bringing pain into our lives and keeping us from growing today. We have found that all of us inevitably encounter these feelings, and it only makes matters worse if we deny we have them or try to will them away. Step ten allows us to recognize our emotions and walk through the pain they cause us, but then to let go of them, and turn them over to our Higher Power so that we can regain our emotional balance.

In steps five through nine we ventured outside of our isolation to share ourselves in depth with our Higher

Power and with other people. Most of us had spent our lives before OA trying to go it alone. As we worked these steps, we learned how much healing and help there is in loving connections with a Power greater than ourselves and with those who share our lives. We now want to continue strengthening these connections, and we have a way to do that through our practice of step ten.

There are many ways to take personal inventories. The simplest are taken mentally, and some veterans in the twelve-step way of life have become so adept at this practice that self-analysis is second nature. Spot-check inventories, taken whenever we find ourselves facing difficulties, are something we can learn to do in a few moments of quiet reflection whenever the need arises. With practice, it becomes easier to recognize the exact nature of our problems and see what actions we need to take to restore our serenity, actions we will want to carry out "promptly," as step ten advises. Perhaps we've forgotten our step-three decision and are trying to control some aspect of our lives by self-will. Maybe we need to discuss the problem with our sponsor, maybe we need to ask our Higher Power to remove a character defect, or maybe we have wronged someone and now owe amends. Once we begin to practice this pattern of on-the-spot analysis and action whenever we're disturbed, it becomes a habit for us, and we discover we've learned an amazing new set of skills for successful living.

When something more than a spot-check is called

for, many of us have found it helpful to write our step-ten inventories. Putting our thoughts and feelings down on paper or describing a troubling incident helps us to better understand our actions and reactions in a way that is often not revealed to us by simply thinking or talking about them. When we write about our difficulties, it becomes easier to see situations more clearly and perhaps better discern any actions that need to be taken.

Some of us make a daily habit of reviewing our emotions and behavior of the past twenty-four hours. A more leisurely and careful analysis than the spot-check inventory, a daily inventory may be written or done mentally. Its purpose is to reveal those areas in which we're having difficulties in our daily lives and help us determine what we can do about them. It also serves as a reminder of those things which are going well for us and for which we might be grateful. There are several ways in which daily inventories may be done. Some of us simply review the major events of the day in chronological order, making note of the feelings we had and how we dealt with those feelings. Some of us draw up a balance sheet, listing negative feelings and events on one side, and positive feelings and events on the other. Some of us work from a list of common character defects and their opposites such as fear/faith, resentment/acceptance, greed/generosity, and so on. Referring to this list, we ask ourselves such questions as: "What fears did I experience today, and how did I react to them?" Then we list or recall those instances when we became aware that our former defects had been removed; when we acted on faith; when we were accepting and forgiving, letting go of former resentments; when we were selfless; or when we exhibited other positive character traits.

In taking daily inventory, we seek to become increasingly aware of our true motives and emotions. We seek to examine our actions so we can learn from our mistakes and build on our successes. Our purpose is not to stir up negative feelings and guilt, but to continue along the path of progress and to recognize those areas of our lives in which progress is being made.

After we have taken our daily inventory, we can follow through with the second half of step ten which says, "when we were wrong, promptly admitted it." This simple little clause implies that we have the opportunity to do more than just look at our defects and assets. We can take the same actions with them that we did with the character traits we found in our fourth-step inventory: discuss them with our Higher Power and, perhaps, another person; turn the defects over, asking our Higher Power to remove them; and make amends where they are due. Some OAs make a daily call to a sponsor in which we read or discuss the tenth-step inventory. We discuss our problems and successes with our Higher Power in prayer as well, daily asking for help to let go of defects and expressing gratitude when we discover that defects are removed and problems resolved. Inevitably, there are those times when we make mistakes and harm other people. Step ten suggests that we make amends *promptly,* as soon as we realize someone has been wronged. By doing this, we bring a new honesty into our relationships. We find we can save ourselves days of resentment and fear by resolving disputes as they arise, instead of allowing wounds to fester.

A tenth-step inventory can also be more extensive, similar to the one we took in step four but dealing with problems we may not have been aware of when we originally took the fourth step. A need to re-inventory some aspects of our past does not mean we failed to do step four properly. It simply shows that we have grown in self-awareness and have become ready to face and resolve aspects of our lives which we were not capable of dealing with the first time around. Each of us is an individual with individual needs, and no two of us proceed at exactly the same pace or work this program in exactly the same way.

An extensive tenth-step inventory might focus on one particular character defect, behavior pattern, or area of life. We will probably want to write this inventory, as we did the fourth step, and we will certainly want to follow through with prompt action. As soon as possible we will want to give this inventory away to another person. After this we will repeat the actions of steps six and seven, asking our Higher Power to heal our wounds, remove any defects we have discovered in our investigation, and help us change our behavior. Then we'll complete this course of action by listing and making any amends we might owe in connection with events listed in this inventory.

A persistent effort to let go of our defects and change our actions will be crucial to our recovery from here on. As we become aware of shortcomings through the inventory process, there are several actions we can take to be rid of them. One such action would be to imagine how we might behave if we did not have a particular defect. We could picture ourselves in the circumstances where we have acted out our shortcoming, but see ourselves acting differently this time. Anything we can imagine, we can do, with the help of our Higher Power. We might even speak the new words or act out the improved set of behaviors, just for practice. Through this kind of action, we daily affirm to ourselves that we can change and are changing, with God's help. At first we may slip back into the old ways in moments of pressure, but we won't let this discourage us. We've spent a lifetime learning to do things the old ways, so of course the old behaviors will feel much more natural to us at first. As time goes on, however, God will help us let go of our defects and replace them with positive habits of thinking and acting. God will, that is, if we persist in doing whatever we can to change.

As with the fourth-step inventory, the tenth-step inventory may uncover aspects of our past with which we need professional help. Our OA friends are sympathetic and loving, but few are trained to recognize and deal with deeply rooted psychological problems, and OA is not the place to seek such help.

As we repeatedly act on step ten, we begin to see the remarkable way the steps will, from now on, continue to remove unnecessary turmoil and pain from our lives. The new attitudes of honesty about our problems and surrender to a Power greater than ourselves have become a part of us by now; they are the basis of every choice we make in our day-to-day lives. Reviewing our recent behavior, keeping our Higher Power in charge of our lives, asking for guidance, and promptly admitting our errors, becomes a sane and satisfying way of life—far better than nursing our fears or building a fresh set of resentments to harbor. Forced to adopt this new way of coping with life in order to recover from compulsive eating, we now find ourselves grateful for this program in its own right. Practicing the program has given us many gifts—gifts which we wouldn't trade for the quick-and-easy solutions to our compulsive eating many of us once sought in every new diet. More gifts are in store for us as we continue working the program and experiencing the miracle of permanent recovery, one day at a time.

*Sought through prayer and meditation to improve our conscious contact with God **as we understood Him**, praying only for knowledge of His will for us and the power to carry that out.*

When we began attending meetings of Overeaters Anonymous, most of us were attracted by the unconditional acceptance we experienced here, a love which has continued to sustain us as we've worked the steps and faced the changes that have come about in our lives as a result. Now, as we encounter step eleven, we are challenged to seek out more direct conscious contact with the ultimate source of that life-changing love.

In OA we share a belief that we can each recover through a spiritual relationship with a Power which is greater than ourselves alone. While based on this shared belief, our program does not promote or favor any particular concept of the exact nature of this Power. In OA meetings we often hear the power source called "my Higher Power," or, more succinctly, "H.P." This can be disconcerting to newcomers, but for those who've been around long enough to work through the first ten steps, the term "Higher Power" signals a freedom we've come to appreciate and even treasure—the freedom to encounter this healing force directly and express our beliefs however we choose. In order to recover from compulsive eating, we need a living, developing, ongoing relationship with this Higher Power, and we find having complete freedom to seek that relationship is a vital aspect of our program.

It takes more than spiritual freedom, however, to establish and develop a relationship with a Power greater than ourselves. We have to take action. In step eleven we are challenged to actively seek to improve our relationship with our Higher Power in the same way we might develop any relationship, by taking the time on a regular basis to be with H.P. Most of us have found it necessary to set aside some time each day when we can be alone and undisturbed. During this time we will actively seek to develop a consciousness of our power source through prayer and meditation, and to do so with an attitude of complete trust, asking only for knowledge of the directions we are to take and for power to move ahead.

We may feel awkward about regular daily prayer at first. Step eleven encourages us to *practice* prayer, to continue talking to our Higher Power daily, even when it seems like a senseless exercise. All of us who have utilized step eleven, consistently giving a part of each day to meditation and prayer, have been rewarded— and sometimes awed—by the results. For many of us a regular daily quiet time for prayer and meditation is essential, a part of this program we don't want to live without, for it gives us the direction and strength we need to live the rest of that day effectively. Many of us begin our day with prayer and meditation, end it with another time of prayer and meditation, and also use these practices at all times during the day when we feel the need for guidance, strength, or serenity.

Step eleven's suggestions are not intended to interfere with or replace the traditional religious practices some of us follow. Rather, we have found that these suggestions enhance the practice of our chosen religion. At the same time, neither step eleven nor any other step requires us to adopt an organized religion.

As with so many other aspects of this program, there is no one right way to do step eleven. "Keep it simple" is a good slogan to apply here. Remembering that our goal is to develop a closer conscious contact with God, prayer is simply what we do when we talk with our Higher Power, and meditation is simply a way of stilling our minds and opening our spirits to God's influence.

What do we say when we talk with God? We say whatever we feel like saying. Some of us begin to practice prayer by reciting prayers we have memorized, perhaps prayers we've read in program literature or other books, learned in meetings, or remember from childhood. There are many wonderful prayers available that over the centuries have nourished those seeking spiritual growth. As we say these prayers day after day and think about their meaning for us in our present circumstances, we are beginning to practice meditation as well, though we may not realize it. As we fix our attention on the truths contained in these prayers, we open our minds to receive new understanding and direction from our Higher Power.

In addition to repeating memorized prayers, we can express ourselves to God in our own words, much as we might talk with our best friend. Some of us have been taught that there are things we shouldn't say to God or feelings we shouldn't express. However, now that we're recovering from compulsive eating, we need complete freedom to express our honest feelings in any situation, without fear of saying the wrong thing and damaging or destroying our relationship with God. Such freedom is an essential factor in the healing process because recovery is based on the practice of honesty with ourselves and our Higher Power. We need the security that comes from knowing that nothing can destroy our relationship with this all-important source of healing and strength while we honestly explore our deepest selves.

The eleventh step guides us to ask only for knowledge of God's will for us and the power to carry that out. Since we have turned our will and lives over to the care of this Higher Power, it makes little sense for us to spend our prayer time giving God instructions. Does this mean we are never to discuss our needs and problems in prayer, never express our feelings, fears, or desires? Clearly, if we are to develop a vital relationship with a Higher Power, we will need to bring into our prayers all the things that concern us. We pray about these things, not so we can get our way, but so we can bring our will regarding them into alignment with God's will.

All of us who seek to develop a relationship with a Higher Power through prayer experience times when we feel angry with God. Perhaps in the past our reaction to this anger has been to pretend it didn't exist, denying our anger to God and to ourselves. Or perhaps we reacted by giving up on prayer entirely. As we seek to recover with God's help, neither of those options will work for us any longer. So we go ahead and express our anger, but we keep on talking to God. The anger passes, answers come, and we find that we have drawn closer to our Higher Power through this experience.

Many of us have found that the practice of writing down our angry feelings or other concerns in letters to God is a great help. As we write, we clarify issues, we express our feelings honestly, and we communicate with our Higher Power in a way that is very tangible to us. OAs have been known to deliver prayer letters to God in all sorts of ways. We've mailed them to our sponsor, put them in a can we've labeled our "God can," made a burnt offering of them, hung them on a tree branch, or dropped them in the river. Such private rituals often seemed silly to us at first, but we've found they work wonders. The key is that we've stopped worrying, taken an action, and turned our problems over to our Higher Power. Our energies are no longer bound up in our worries and resentments, and we are free to move forward again, to do God's will.

Meditation is our way of quieting our minds so we

can get better acquainted with this Higher Power of ours. As with prayer, there is no one right way to practice meditation; in fact, most of us vary our practices from time to time. The only way to do meditation wrong is not to do it at all. We compulsive people are oriented to action. Meditation is an action which gives us much-needed practice in the art of sitting still and opening our hearts to receive spiritual nourishment. Many of us have spent a lot of time running—running from the food, then running to it—and many of us have turned to excess food for its sedative effect. Eating compulsively was our chief means of relaxation. Meditation offers us a way to stop running and to relax without eating.

When meditating, we consciously choose to focus our minds on something other than our everyday desires and concerns. We might begin to do this by breathing deeply and counting our breaths, by holding a special object and concentrating on how it feels, by listening to soft music, by repeating a word or phrase, by concentrating on an image, by staring at an object or picture, or by other means. When we are distracted by worries or annoyances, we will gently let go of these distractions and return our attention to consideration of the truths with which we are asking God to fill our minds. Our purpose in meditating is simple: we seek to relax and receive spiritual nourishment by experiencing more fully our connections with our true unfragmented selves and with our Higher Power.

Step eleven implies that through our practice of prayer and meditation we will come to know God's will for us. Here the question arises: how, exactly, are we to know which thoughts are God's directions and which are our own rationalizations? A communication from God might be difficult for us to recognize at first because it probably won't come in audible words. Instead, it may come in the form of a new idea or concept, it may come as a change in our motives or attitudes, or it may simply be a feeling we have that our energy has been renewed or our bad mood has lifted. We can recognize a communication from our Higher Power by the effect it has on us. If time spent in prayer and meditation makes us even a little bit saner or more loving, if it encourages or strengthens us even a tiny bit, we can be sure God has "spoken" and we have "heard."

Our sponsors and other OAs with experience in prayer and meditation can also help us recognize God's direction. When we believe we have received insight from our Higher Power, we find it wise to discuss the matter with our sponsor or spiritual advisor before we take any drastic action. There will be times when we're faced with an important decision and want to know our Higher Power's will. Our sponsor or OA friend might suggest that we pray about it, asking God to increase our desire to take the action if we are supposed to take it, or decrease our desire if we're not supposed to take it. After this prayer we stop worrying about making the decision right now and we wait a day or so, meanwhile keeping our eyes, ears, and minds open. By the end of the waiting period we will inevitably find that we've gained a clearer perspective on the decision. Despite our most sincere efforts, we sometimes make an error in acting on what we think is God's will for us. In time we may be grateful for the lessons we have learned in these situations. It is through such experiences that we grow more adept at recognizing the will of our Higher Power in the future.

OAs who have made prayer and meditation a regular part of their lives have found a resource for healing and strength which cannot fail. Sponsors, OA friends, meetings, and literature are wonderful sources of help for us. We wouldn't want to be without any of these resources because we often find God speaks to us through them. From time to time, however, each of them will fail us in a moment of need. Our Higher Power is the only source of help that is always available to us, always strong enough to lift us up and set our feet on the path of life. Prayer and meditation are our links to this unfailing source. Practiced regularly, they open our lives to the comfort we sought in food but could never find. Through prayer and meditation we align ourselves with a higher spiritual Power which gives us everything we need to live to our fullest potential.

Having had a spiritual awakening as the result of these steps, we tried to carry this message to compulsive overeaters and to practice these principles in all our affairs.

Step twelve begins with the acknowledgment of a great truth: We who have worked the first eleven steps of the Overeaters Anonymous program have had a spiritual awakening, and we now have a message of hope to carry to other compulsive overeaters. We who once suffered from complete powerlessness to control our eating and our lives have now discovered the saving strength of a Power greater than ourselves. We have experienced the miracle of physical, emotional, and spiritual healing, just as we were promised when we began these steps.

For most of us, the central factor in this spiritual awakening has been our decision to trust a Higher Power with every aspect of our lives. In acting on that decision one day at a time, we have learned a whole new set of skills for living, skills which enable us to clear from our lives everything which might interfere with our trust in this Higher Power. Now we know we don't have to fear anything that comes to us. Even when things happen to us which we don't like, we know we have a way of facing each situation squarely and sanely. We have seen that our Higher Power will reveal something of value to us with every experience, as long as we continue practicing this new way of life.

We're no longer afraid of food, either, because we are no longer controlled by it. The glorious fact for most of us is that God has lifted the food obsession from us. Freed of the obsession and restored to sanity, today we choose not to eat self-destructively. We have new ways of coping with our problems now and new practices which make living a positive, joyful experience most of the time. If we should again crave more food than we need, we know we will find relief in the steps instead of in compulsive eating.

This being true, are we now ready to complete the twelfth step and graduate from OA? Looking back at how far we've come, many of us have been tempted to think we've arrived at the end of the journey. The truth, learned from the experiences of thousands of OAs, is that even when we've reached a goal of health, body size, or weight; even when we've worked all twelve steps to the best of our ability; even when we've celebrated milestone anniversaries of abstinence and recovery; even when we've been placed in positions of trust by other OAs and have rendered service on the group, intergroup, regional, and international levels; we still haven't arrived. The twelfth step invites us to continue the journey one day at a time for the rest of our lives. We need to keep moving forward in recovery, keep developing our spiritual consciousness, if we are to remain spiritually awake and fully alive.

Perhaps it is fortunate for us, and for the millions

of compulsive overeaters who still suffer, that most of us who've worked this program will be unable to keep the recovery we have unless we share our experience, strength, and hope with others. Some of us have tried to follow our program in isolation and have been unable to keep our emotional balance and our abstinence. Had this been possible, we might not be here today to carry the message to newcomers. We would have missed the best part of the twelve steps, for the greatest joy of recovery comes to us when we share our OA program with others.

Few of us suspected this would be so when we started working the steps. For years we've looked for gratification in unbridled eating; in material possessions; in careers; in our many attempts to have perfect bodies; and in money, sex, and social status. Although most of us have received and enjoyed some of these things, the satisfaction we felt in them was small compared with the joy we have found in sharing this program with other compulsive overeaters.

Service in OA has been a surprisingly powerful factor in our recovery. Simple actions which seemed unimportant when we took them have turned out to have profound effects on us and on others. Hugs we've given at meetings, phone calls we've made, letters we've written, simple words of encouragement which we've spoken and quickly forgotten, have come back to us—sometimes at the very moment we've needed them most—from people who received through them the strength to keep walking the OA path. Most of us who have been around OA for more than a few months have seen miracles of recovery in our meetings. We count among our friends people whom we first met when they were suffering newcomers. We've seen them transformed by this simple program, and we are gratified to have played our part, even if all we did was show up at OA meetings and say, "Keep coming back!" The joy we receive as we try to carry the message is a positive force in our lives today, sustaining us through good times and hard times, transforming us and our companions in recovery.

Talking about OA with those who still suffer has become an increasingly natural thing for us to do. Sometimes because of the changes in our bodies, and sometimes because of the changes in our attitudes, people now say to us: "You look wonderful! What have you done?" It becomes easier and easier to mention our involvement in OA, to share more of what we've experienced here, to invite friends to join us.

We usually ask God to help us in talking about the program with those outside OA and with those in meetings. When we turn ourselves over to our Higher Power, we can relax and speak honestly without worrying that we might not say the right thing. Also, we've found it less confusing to others if we make it a habit when sharing about the program to concentrate on our OA experience, rather than on aspects of our experience not related to OA. Though we may have been helped by therapies, church attendance, food plans, exercise programs, self-help books, metaphysics, and the like, we've found it best to emphasize our experience with the twelve steps, which are the basis of recovery for all of us.

We've also found that service has worked out best for us when we had no expectations regarding the outcome. When we set out to fix other people, we usually failed, despite lavishing long hours on them. Nor do we need to devise plans for saving the whole world in order to work step twelve. God finds many ways to help people through us as long as we are willing to do what we can, when we can, and keep ourselves on the path of spiritual progress.

The twelfth step suggests that we continue to practice our new way of acting upon life "in all our affairs," and the vast experience of recovering compulsive overeaters confirms the importance of this suggestion. As we've worked the first eleven steps, the principles embodied in them have begun to replace our old way of life, which centered on self and compulsive eating. In step twelve we confirm that we have turned our backs on the old ways forever. We are moving in a new direction of spiritual growth.

What are some of the principles inherent in each step that we are encouraged to practice in all our affairs? In step one we learned the principle of *honesty* as we admitted our personal powerlessness over food, and the fact that without help we could not successfully manage our own lives. Now we will want to continue being honest with ourselves in all our affairs. One important way in which we practice honesty today is by admitting that we are still compulsive overeaters, that we still need daily help.

In step two we learned *hope* as we came to believe that a Power greater than ourselves could restore us to sanity. This same hope will now need to underlie all our actions. Even in our loneliest hours, we can remind ourselves of the great truth that we are not alone; even in our weakest moments we will find the strength we need if we believe it is available to us and ask for it.

In step three we learned *faith* as we made the most important decision we had ever made, the decision to trust God—as we understand God—with our will and our lives. Practicing the principle of faith today means that we will no longer go through life acting however we feel like acting at any given moment. Instead we will look to our Higher Power for guidance and strength as we face each decision.

In steps four and five we learned *courage* and *integrity* as we faced the truth about our defects of character. Applying these principles in all our affairs means that we are no longer ruled by a fear of admitting our mistakes. We have the integrity to show the world our true selves. No longer needing to appear to the world as perfect people, we can live more fully, having the courage to face up to our mistakes and test our strengths in the challenges of life.

In step six we learned more about the necessity of *willingness* as we became entirely ready to let go of our shortcomings. We apply this principle in many ways now, learning through each day's experience the difference between self-will and a simple willingness to cooperate with the guidance of our Higher Power.

In step seven we began to understand the meaning of *humility*. We practice this principle today by continuing to let go of status-seeking and of thoughts and actions by which we belittled ourselves and others, and to humbly trust God for the removal of our shortcomings.

In steps eight and nine we looked at the damage we had done others and set about repairing it. Now we apply the same principles of *self-discipline* and *love* for others to all of our actions. Self-discipline makes us less likely to hurt other people and quicker to make amends when we do. Practicing the principle of love we learn to accept others as they are, not as we would have them be. We're beginning to take this new attitude not just toward other OAs, but also toward those at home, school, work, and in all areas of our lives. Slowly but surely we find we are establishing the best possible relationship with each person we know.

In step ten we discovered the value of *perseverance* in working the twelve steps. Practicing this principle in all our affairs today means that we continue to do the things which have brought us healing, even though we sometimes wonder if we still need to. Perseverance brings us the reward of continuing, permanent recovery.

In step eleven we learned the principle of *spiritual awareness* as we turned our attention to the practices of prayer and meditation. We practice this principle by seeking an awareness of God's presence in all our affairs, and by continuing to nurture our spiritual sensitivity through prayer and meditation.

The principle of *service* which underlies OA's twelfth step can now guide our actions both inside and outside the program. Here we experience the great truth that when we let go of our need to control people and simply allow our Higher Power to serve others through us, we receive an abundance of joy and strength.

We who began working the steps in order to recover from compulsive eating now find that through them we have embarked on a lifelong journey of spiritual growth. From the isolation of food obsession we have emerged into a new world. Walking hand in hand with our friends and our Higher Power, we are now exploring this world, using the great spiritual principles embodied in the twelve steps as the map to guide our way. We gratefully follow in the footsteps of many others who have walked this way before us, and we're gratified to be making footprints of our own for others to follow.

Those of us who live this program don't simply carry the message; *we are the message.* Each day that we live well, we *are* well, and we embody the joy of recovery which attracts others who want what we've found in OA. We're always happy to share our secret: the twelve steps of Overeaters Anonymous, which empower each of us to live well and be well, one day at a time.

Introduction To
The Twelve Traditions

When we first came to Overeaters Anonymous we were focused on our own recovery. Most of us took for granted the OA group we attended and the OA Fellowship as a whole, not thinking much about how they operated and whether they would continue to be there for us in the future. Soon, however, as we left behind our dependence on food, we began to rely on OA. We felt it was our only safe haven, and we reacted with fear any time we thought this Fellowship might be threatened.

Yet we quickly found that we did not need to be afraid for the health of OA. Overeaters Anonymous has twelve traditions which are designed to keep our meetings and service committees on track, functioning in such a way as to nurture the recovery of all compulsive overeaters who seek help in this Fellowship. This study of the traditions shows how these twelve suggestions have worked to help individuals, groups, and OA as a whole solve problems, thrive, and be effective instruments for carrying the message of recovery to those who still suffer.

We owe a large debt of gratitude to Alcoholics Anonymous for breaking ground in establishing these traditions and allowing OA to adapt them to our Fellowship. Developed through long and sometimes painful experience, the twelve traditions embody the same principles for living as do the twelve steps. Those who have studied them carefully have found that these traditions can be applied effectively to all human relationships, both inside and outside OA. With this in mind, we turn our attention to the traditions, trusting that as we come to understand them better, we will be better able to keep our OA lifeboat afloat and ourselves spiritually fit in the face of all challenges.

Our common welfare should come first; personal recovery depends upon OA unity.

We compulsive overeaters have lived most of our lives in isolation. Many of us preferred to be alone so we could overeat without interference. Even when we were surrounded by other people, it became progressively difficult for us to connect with them as our obsession with food, body size, and eating grew. Some of us felt like failures whenever we had to seek help from anyone outside ourselves.

Our desire to live free of compulsive eating has forced us to change these attitudes. Recovery began for most of us when we got out of isolation and into an OA group. Here we discovered we were never meant to live alone. As we opened our hearts to other OA members, we found acceptance, a sense of belonging, and unity with other compulsive overeaters that satisfied us in ways food never could.

Many of us would not be alive today if it were not for our OA groups. Here is the only place we have found recovery from the devastating disease of compulsive eating. If we are to continue to live and recover, we must have the continued support of OA groups and the inspiration of our fellow OA members. What's more, we need daily opportunities to be of service to other compulsive overeaters, opportunities which the OA group provides.

Thus, the unity of OA is a matter of life and death to us. However, unity isn't always easy to maintain. OA members come from diverse backgrounds, and in meetings we sometimes encounter people very different from us in their approaches to recovery. Often, our first impulse is to insist they are doing it all wrong. If we as individuals did not value the common welfare of the Fellowship above our own personal viewpoints, OA would soon split into argumentative factions, and would lose the strength that comes from our union of many.

In OA meetings, individuals are lovingly guided to keep the needs of the whole group in mind as we share our experience, strength, and hope. Because all OA groups do not have the same meeting format, we often begin our meetings with such statements as "no cross talk, please" or "three-minute positive pitches" or "this is a nonsmoking meeting" to tell everybody in attendance what the group conscience is. A respect for unity means that individuals keep in mind the ground rules of the group. We may want to talk for longer than the prescribed three minutes, or we may feel that we "just have to share" our advice with someone in a meeting. Tradition one tells us to curb those impulses for the sake of the group.

Usually our meeting formats are geared to keep our groups' practices in line with OA principles.

Ideally, OA is a place where every member has ample opportunity to share, where we don't try to confront or fix each other in the groups, where we do not dump the most intimate details of our lives on the meetings, but save them for one-on-one discussions with our sponsors. It is every member's responsibility to protect the OA spirit of unity and mutual support. And, when it comes our turn to lead an OA meeting, tradition one makes it our responsibility to lovingly remind individuals of the group's guidelines whenever the group conscience is being ignored.

This does not mean that all OA members must agree on every issue regarding the operation of the Fellowship. Disagreements about the activities of the group arise every day, and we have to find ways of resolving those disagreements without destroying the unity of our Fellowship. What tradition one suggests is that we give other people's opinions a respectful hearing. We express our own opinions honestly without belittling those who may disagree. As we listen and speak, we keep our minds and hearts open to our Higher Power's will in all matters. After the discussion is over and the group has made a decision, we don't allow any lingering feelings of conflict to divide the group. In OA, we resolve our differences of opinion by considering the welfare of the group as a whole.

Through experience OA groups have learned the importance of unity. In one city, a personality conflict divided the intergroup. Two factions squared off as each advocated its own concept of recovery. When months of arguments had brought no resolution, one faction formed a new intergroup.

A short time later, when people on both sides had achieved a degree of tranquility, the OA regional organization encouraged the two intergroups to host a regionwide OA convention. Neither intergroup had the resources to do the job alone; they were forced to sit down face-to-face and find a way to work together. Individuals within each faction willing to do this formed a First-Tradition Committee, the purpose of which was to find a basis for unity. Changes in attitudes would be needed if the two intergroups were to hold together long enough to stage the convention. Because they wanted to work together, the members of the committee began to focus on the principles they could agree upon, rather than on their differences, and finally they came up with a single group conscience. In a joint statement, both intergroups recognized the existence of various recovery approaches within the OA Fellowship. Both recognized that a common need brought them together. They stated that manners of working the program were clearly matters of personal or group conscience, and they agreed to refrain from comment or discussion on their differences.

By respecting those guidelines, the two factions found they could indeed work together to stage a successful OA convention. A decade later, neither intergroup had changed its philosophy on how to work the OA program, and yet both were still flourishing, still holding conventions and Unity Day celebrations together, still very active in OA regional and World Service events. Each supported many strong OA groups where individuals found recovery through the twelve steps.

Members of the only OA group in a tiny midwestern town had a similar conflict and found their way to unity as well. Meetings were attended by fewer than ten people, and as with many small OA groups, one or two who had several years in the program kept the meetings going. One night an OA who had recently moved to town showed up and told a dramatic story about her near death from compulsive eating. She described how she had found OA in California and how OA and a food plan had saved her life.

The small-town OA members were very impressed when this woman told them about her weight loss in excess of 100 pounds, and were inspired by the light in her eyes and her obvious enthusiasm for the program. One person, however, who was the group's mainstay got nervous when the transferred member talked about her food plan. The mainstay herself had experienced a miraculous recovery from compulsive eating, and she believed part of that miracle was that she had been freed from years of compulsive dieting and food planning. She used her discussion time to speak against the transferred member's food plan.

Within weeks factions had formed around the mainstay and the transferred member, and heated arguments about the use of the food plan dominated the meeting. This went on for several months with very hard feelings on both sides.

Then, one night in late summer, the mainstay and the transferred member found themselves the only two people to show up for the weekly OA meeting. After waiting for ten minutes for a third person to arrive, they finally agreed to start the meeting with just the two of them. Together they said the Serenity Prayer and began to follow the meeting format. Sitting face-to-face across the table, they took turns discussing their experience, strength, and hope. Little by little their sharing became more honest. The mainstay found herself admitting to the transferred member how much she envied her recovery, and how she'd felt upstaged. The transferred member talked with tears in her eyes of how scared she was of relapse, how she'd wanted to start a group like her old home group in California, but hadn't been able to find anybody else willing to join her. More than anything, she said, she needed understanding and support. She longed for the mainstay's strength and admired her experience with OA principles.

Before the meeting was over, the transferred member and the mainstay had agreed to sponsor each other. When other group members returned to OA the following week, they found a whole new atmosphere. The transferred member hadn't given up her food plan and the mainstay hadn't adopted it. They still had differing goals for their eating, but they now expressed support for each other in reaching those goals. Even more striking was the new note of love and acceptance in their voices when they shared their reasons for sticking with their differing approaches to abstinence. When some group members decided to use the food plan, the mainstay didn't try to dissuade them. When other people followed the philosophy of the mainstay, the transferred member didn't argue. They had found there was room for more than one approach to recovery in this little group.

Unity does not mean uniformity. In OA we learn we can disagree with other people on important issues and still be supportive friends. We listen to others with open minds, and we learn to express ourselves without insisting that everyone must do things our way. As we practice these new skills we begin to better understand ourselves and others. It becomes easier to find ways of doing things which meet everybody's needs.

How well do we practice the principle of unity? We might ask ourselves a few questions about how we act in our OA groups:

Is our group dividing into cliques and being indifferent to some members?

Do we seek to pull together as a group, or are we divisive? Do we discourage gossip? Do we discourage members from taking each others' inventories?

Do we focus on what we have in common, or do we bring up our differences, just for the sake of argument?

Are we kind, even to those whose personalities we dislike? Or do we talk about the love of the OA group while acting hostile to some?

Do we encourage everybody to give full attention to speakers and other group members who are speaking to the group? Or do side conversations or greetings often distract from the OA meeting?

Does our group encourage members to speak briefly, or do we allow some to dominate discussions by speaking so much that others don't get their turns?

Do those leading our meetings allow newcomers to dominate the discussion or interrupt others, or do we help them to be a part of the group right away by telling them about the meeting format and ground rules in a kind way?

Do we encourage members to use the telephone to help ourselves and each other, not just for complaints and gossip?

Do we belittle other OA members or groups whose approaches to working the program are different from ours?

Do we support OA activities that bring us into contact with other groups?

Have we taken the time to learn about OA as a whole? Do we support OA as a whole to the best of our ability?

Do we encourage all of our members to share honestly with the group, even when they're going through rough times? Or do we take the attitude that those who are having trouble shouldn't share?

The first tradition of unity reminds us of an important truth: We are not alone. We are connected to our fellow human beings. Our emotional and spiritual health depends upon the health of our relationships. The disease of compulsive eating which once isolated us has now led us to OA. Here, in local groups, sponsorship roles, intergroups, regional assemblies, and OA worldwide, we are learning to connect with other people in ways that will nurture them and nurture us as we recover together.

For our group purpose there is but one ultimate authority—a loving God as He may express Himself in our group conscience. Our leaders are but trusted servants; they do not govern.

The newcomer may ask, "Who is the head of OA?" and be puzzled by the answer in tradition two: a loving God as expressed in the group conscience. The second tradition of Overeaters Anonymous may seem thoroughly impractical, but it works. When faced with a problem or challenge, we ask God's guidance to show us what is best for the group as a whole. Then we discuss the matter carefully, we vote on alternatives, and we trust that the decision we reach together is our Higher Power's will.

It is an axiom of human society that wherever there is a power structure there will be power struggles. This seems to be true even in organizations made up of well-intentioned, idealistic members. Many of us, when placed in a position to do so, will fight for mastery over our fellows even as we speak earnestly in favor of equality. In OA, however, there are no powerful offices to hold. Instead of a power structure, we have a service structure. The offices or boards found in OA exist only to do service. They have no power to enforce rules on other OA groups or individual members. In OA groups, members are chosen to perform services such as keeping track of and distributing the group's money, finding speakers, attending intergroup, or restocking the literature table. OA groups normally spend very little regular meeting time with group business. If somebody wants to make a change in the way a group is operating—to find a new meeting place, for instance, or to use some of the group's funds in a new way—this is brought up for discussion at a business meeting of all the group's regular members. Some groups hold such meetings in conjunction with the regular meeting, and some hold them separately. The informed group conscience decides what action is to be taken and individuals act for the group to implement this decision.

The group conscience is not the same as majority rule. This conscience is an expression of the group unity spoken of in the first tradition, a common bond which grows among us as we each let go of self-will. Rather than being guided by individual self-interest, we seek as a group to apply the principles embodied in OA's steps and traditions to the decision at hand.

In order to reach an *informed* group conscience, we affirm each group member's right to take part in the discussions, and we listen to everyone attentively with open minds. The purpose of our discussions is to make sure that the decision reached by the group takes into account all pertinent information. If we are to reach an informed decision, the group will need to take into account everybody's needs and ideas. For this reason, OA groups give all viewpoints a full hearing— even minority viewpoints.

Nobody who considers herself or himself a group member is excluded from speaking or voting. Since, according to the third OA tradition, "The only requirement for OA membership is a desire to stop eating compulsively," most OA groups do not place abstinence or other requirements on voting rights. How can we trust our group decisions if we allow people to vote who are eating compulsively and might not be clearheaded? This is certainly a danger, but it must be weighed against the need to keep OA open to all who want what our Fellowship has to offer. To exclude some from speaking or voting on decisions for the group denies them effective membership in the group, membership which can be essential to recovery from our "disease of isolation."

Those who have long-term experience with OA groups and traditions have more than a right to speak up; they have a responsibility to share what they have learned. Sometimes what they have to say may be unpopular, and they may hesitate to "rock the boat." Still, the experience of other OA groups and the traditions of OA need to be made known to all of us if we are to act wisely under the authority of a loving God.

Once all voices have been lovingly heard, a group conscience vote is taken. We each base our vote on what we believe is best for the group, not on the personalities of those supporting a particular viewpoint, nor on what our closest friends believe.

In light of tradition two, nobody ever "loses" a group conscience vote in OA. Those of us whose opinions differed from the group decision may be disappointed and angry at first. In the long run, however, we often come to believe that the outcome was a good thing for us personally, as well as for OA. Whether we ever feel this way or not, the reality is that we all win when God's will is done.

Not all our group decisions will be wise and practical. We do make mistakes sometimes and have to look for better answers to a problem. Another group conscience vote can be taken when something needs to be corrected. Like individuals, OA groups learn from their mistakes—and so does OA as a whole. We find that our Higher Power often leads us through our blunders.

Members who have been around long enough to learn from such experiences are sometimes tempted to think their opinions should govern their groups, despite tradition two. When they try to control rather than to serve other members, however, things usually go wrong.

In starting a brand-new OA group, one or a few people might have to make all the decisions at first, but very soon the group conscience takes over the leadership function. The counsel of longtime members continues to be valuable, but it is not good for the group or its leaders if one person holds a particular service position too long. A vital part of our personal growth in OA is giving service, but it is also vital to practice humility by giving up our service office after a specified length of time so someone else can have this opportunity to carry the OA message.

Thus, service positions are rotated regularly in OA groups, even when the person holding the position has done a good job and would be willing to continue. This is somewhat disconcerting to the newcomer who may have taken it for granted that those performing services were in charge of the OA meeting. The first time a group secretary or program chairperson steps down from the position, a newcomer may feel as if the group is falling apart or being deserted by its leadership. After the newcomer returns to the meeting month after month, however, he or she begins to find security in the way the meeting is guided through its group conscience. Eventually, the member who regularly attends a meeting will decide to take part in group conscience discussions and decisions, will find that the group continues to nurture his or her recovery despite changes, and will see opportunities to give service. We take turns filling service offices in OA in the same way that family members might take turns doing household chores.[1]

All OA members share a responsibility for the operation of OA. Sometimes members who don't yet understand how our Fellowship works will be heard to say things like, "Why did they change my favorite pamphlet?" or "Why don't they have a meeting in my hometown?" We soon learn that there is no "they" and "them" in OA, only *we* and *us*. Acting through

1. The *Group Handbook* (Overeaters Anonymous, Inc., 1986) offers many useful suggestions for OA groups and is available from the World Service Office.

literature committees made up of OA members from around the world, *we* decide what literature to publish, rewrite, or discontinue. If *we* want a meeting in town, it's up to those of *us* who want it there to start one. This kind of responsibility sometimes scares us, until we remember the words of tradition two. All we have to do is the footwork, and we can trust the outcome to our loving Higher Power who provides us with all the resources we need.

This book itself is an example of how the second tradition works in OA. Before it was finished, approved by OA's World Service Business Conference, and published in its final form, the OA Fellowship went through a 13-year process in which we discussed—rather heatedly, at times—whether or not there was a need for the book and how it should be written. The text went through three major drafts and numerous revisions incorporating suggestions and comments from hundreds of OA members all over the world.

Several times during those years the entire project seemed doomed by controversy and confusion. Portions of the book were debated and voted on at World Service Business Conferences in 1987, 1989, 1990, 1992, and 1993 before the book was finally approved in its present form. During all these years, many of us wondered if a loving God as expressed in our group conscience could ever really get the book published. Each time, however, a series of events (often unexpected) would occur to solve the problems and get things back on track.

Many of us have had similar experiences in our home meetings. When a group problem is brought up for discussion, a better solution often arises from the workings of the group conscience than from any proposal the group's leaders are able to come up with on their own. As the discussion progresses, a whole new idea emerges, or, from the back of the room, comes the voice of one of the newer members with a fresh idea for solving the problem. To our amazement, heated controversies which threaten to split the group are resolved, and we discover that the group has actually been strengthened in the process.

How do we live up to the principles of the second tradition in our OA meetings?

Does our group encourage everyone to take an active part in meetings and group conscience discussions?

Before voting on group conscience decisions, does the group take the time to find out as much as it can about the matter and discuss it fully? Do we listen with open minds to everyone's point of view?

Do we ever put pressure on the group to accept the ideas of certain individuals simply because they have been in OA a long time?

Do we feel like we have to save face in group discussions, or can we all go along in good spirit with the group conscience, even if we differed with it in the beginning?

Do we criticize service officers, OA committees, and office workers, or do we support their efforts?

Do we hold our service officers accountable?

Does the group give full attention to the group secretary, intergroup representative, and others making announcements?

Do our group's members volunteer or willingly accept group offices (i.e. secretary, treasurer), or does our group have trouble finding members willing to do service? Do we all offer to help set up, clean up, or do other chores? Do we all—even those who are relatively new in OA and even those who have been around a long time—do what we can?

Many of us come to OA with years of experience trying to operate our families, friendships, or work relationships by power or manipulation. We have been amazed by how well the second tradition works in OA, by what happens when we become willing simply to serve the group and let our Higher Power govern through the group conscience.

We find that most people are willing to cooperate cheerfully with decisions they help to make. Instead of arguing, sulking, nagging, or commanding, we learn in OA to state our needs and desires in an adult way and to let others tell us theirs, expressing our willingness to go along with any decision which takes everyone's needs into account. Anger and bitterness are often replaced by harmony and peace when we treat each person as important and really listen to what everyone has to say. When this happens, a loving God's will is expressing itself through us and through our OA groups.

The only requirement for OA membership is a desire to stop eating compulsively.

Most organizations have a list of qualifications for membership, but in Overeaters Anonymous we have only one requirement: a desire to stop eating compulsively.

No person who has this desire can be barred from any OA group. OA members come from many different backgrounds, races, and religions. We can, and do, have differences in opinions, political views, values, lifestyles, age, gender, sexual orientation, and economic status. A person can never be too overweight, too underweight, or too normal in weight to be an OA member. Newcomers sometimes ask, "What if I only have ten pounds to lose?" The answer is there are no weight requirements of any kind in OA.

Nor is it a membership requirement to have common experiences with the disease of compulsive eating. Some of us have been on many diets, while others of us have never dieted at all. Some of us binged, and some didn't. Some of us fasted. Some of us purged by various methods. We count among our members those who have been eating compulsively since childhood and those who never had a problem with food until their retirement years. All who have experienced the pain of compulsive eating and want to stop are equally welcome here.

In OA we even find a wide range of opinions about the program itself—about the twelve steps, the twelve traditions, and how best to apply them. Nobody is expelled from OA for not working the steps, not getting a sponsor, not respecting the traditions, or not adopting the tools and practices many of us employ.

Does this mean the steps, traditions, and tools are unimportant? No, they are the vital difference between OA and all the other ways we have tried to deal with our compulsive eating. Recovery is a journey, and the twelve-step program is the road we travel together in OA. The purpose of tradition three is to ensure that the road will always be accessible to all who wish to travel it. Thus we say that any two or more compulsive eaters who come together to practice the twelve steps and twelve traditions are considered an OA group, as long as they, as a group, have no other affiliations.

As tradition three implies, a desire to abstain—to refrain from eating compulsively—is at the heart of OA membership. There are many opinions among us about what it means, exactly, to stop eating compulsively. Nobody is excluded from OA membership because of his or her personal opinion of how to achieve abstinence. Note, too, that while the *desire* to stop eating compulsively is required, a person doesn't have to be abstinent to be welcome at OA meetings. We encourage one another to keep coming back, no matter what. In fact, many of us have kept coming back to OA despite problems with abstinence and have found this to be the key to our recovery. In OA the door never closes to a member who has returned to active compulsive eating, and many members who have maintained long-term abstinence had at some time in the past felt themselves to be hopeless because they had trouble staying abstinent or experienced a relapse.

Occasionally groups are plagued by members who disrupt the harmony of the meetings. Even these people are not permanently barred from the group and denied the chance to recover. Of course groups must protect their members from violence or harassment. Groups have been known to confront a person acting in an abusive manner and ask him or her to leave the meeting. Luckily, such extreme cases are rare. We have found that most personality problems can best be dealt with on a one-to-one basis through sponsorship. Our OA meetings aren't always going to be perfect, but we can find recovery in them despite their imperfections. When every person is respected and treated lovingly, the group survives and emerges stronger than ever from the experience.

Over the years, many OA groups have had participation requirements other than the simple desire to stop eating compulsively. In some, for instance, a person had to follow a certain food plan for a certain number of days in order to share in the meeting. In others, a person needed permission from a sponsor to share.

The question arose: Is this not a breach of the

third tradition? If people have to meet special requirements in order to have any voice in the meeting, aren't they being denied effective membership in the group? Generally the group conscience of OA as a whole has agreed with this interpretation of tradition three, but there has been much discussion on this point. After all, the autonomy of groups is also a closely guarded OA tradition, and groups having those kinds of requirements have been vital to the recovery of many of our members.

In votes at the World Service Business Conferences in 1983, 1987, and 1989, delegates sought to formulate a way of dealing with this issue that would protect the autonomy of meetings and at the same time make sure that all compulsive overeaters can feel welcome in our Fellowship. A policy statement they adopted read: "Overeaters Anonymous respects the autonomy of each OA group. We do suggest, however, that any group which imposes a special purpose, task or guideline should inform its members that this special purpose, task or guideline does not represent OA as a whole. The only requirement for membership is the desire to stop eating compulsively. Anyone who says they are a member is a member. We of Overeaters Anonymous welcome all members with open arms."[1]

Some special-requirement meetings still exist within the OA Fellowship. Two examples are special

---

1. *Final Report—Overeaters Anonymous World Service Business Conference* (Overeaters Anonymous, Inc., published annually).

meetings for relapse recovery and step studies at which membership is limited and where participants must commit to attend regularly and complete assignments. Such support can be a boon to the OA member who needs extra help to reinforce his or her program. However, because of their special requirements, these groups are discouraged from registering with our World Service Office.

There are also special-emphasis groups in OA, such as those especially for newcomers, for men, for women, for gays and lesbians, for maintainers, or for bulimics. In cases where these are registered OA groups, they should not exclude any compulsive eater who wants to attend and share, even though the member might not fit the category toward which the meeting is geared.

We don't want to exclude any of our fellow sufferers or create barriers to their recovery. Many of us come to OA feeling like the rest of the world misunderstands compulsive overeaters and our problems. For us, OA is the only place where we truly feel we belong.

How do we live by the principles which underlie OA's third tradition?

Does our group encourage everyone to take part in discussions?

Do we make every type of compulsive eater welcome, or are there some types we would rather not have in OA or in our OA group?

Do we focus our discussions on the things we, as compulsive overeaters, have in common?

Do we let people's age, race, education, manner of dress, weight, religion (or lack of it), political beliefs, language, or other such factors determine whether we will reach out to them in OA meetings and on the phone?

Are we too greatly impressed by a newcomer's celebrity? By professional status? By his or her experience with other twelve-step programs? Or can the group treat each new member just like it would treat any other compulsive eater?

Do we make it a point to speak to newcomers, even when their appearances or attitudes are not inviting? Do we let them know they are welcome in OA?

Does the group continue to extend a welcome to all compulsive eaters, even those who have been critical of group practices in the past?

Before OA, we may have placed special requirements on our friends, coworkers, or family members. "I will love you if . . ." often characterized our attitude toward them. Perhaps we demanded that others live up to our standards or we placed conditions on friendships: "If you disagree with me, you have betrayed me." In OA we've learned that people can differ with us on important matters and still be loving, supportive friends.

When we apply OA's tradition three, we find the treasure of friendship often where we least expect it, with people we once would have excluded from our lives. Such treasure is all around us, and all we have to do is open our hearts to receive it. OA is where we learn to open our hearts, because it is here that most of us first experience unconditional acceptance. "We have a home, if we want it" is how "Our Invitation to You" in the *Overeaters Anonymous* book expresses tradition three. "Welcome to Overeaters Anonymous. Welcome home!"[2]

---

2. *Overeaters Anonymous* (Overeaters Anonymous, Inc., 1980), p. 6.

Each group should be autonomous
except in matters affecting
other groups or OA as a whole.

A favorite saying in Overeaters Anonymous is "There are no musts in this program." As individuals we are responsible for ourselves and free to work (or not work) the twelve-step program however we wish. The same principle holds true for OA groups. Tradition four—the tradition of autonomy—gives OA groups the right and responsibility to operate as they see fit, free from any outside influence. Autonomy means that OA groups can have no affiliations other than with OA. It also means that no other group or service body—even inside OA—can dictate group action. There is only one limit to group autonomy in tradition four: Groups should not do anything which will injure other OA groups or OA as a whole.

Tradition four gives OA groups the freedom to do what works best for them. Each group chooses its own meeting place and time, format and practices. Every OA group makes its own decisions—and mistakes—without interference from any governing body other than its own group conscience.

Because groups are autonomous, OA members who visit meetings away from home often encounter group practices which seem strange to them. "These people aren't doing it right," the visitor thinks. "I miss my home group!" Sooner or later, however, the visitor discovers a delightful truth. OA meetings around the globe are alike in one respect: Every OA group operates in an atmosphere which promotes recovery from compulsive overeating through the twelve steps and twelve traditions.

One very strong reason that all groups are alike in spirit can be found in the second half of tradition four. Autonomy extends only to matters which don't affect other OA groups or OA as a whole. What kinds of matters are likely to affect the entire OA Fellowship?

One instance would be a group which doesn't use the twelve steps and twelve traditions as the basis for its meetings. By calling itself "OA" but not offering OA principles to its members, this group would be misleading compulsive overeaters about the OA program and harming the Fellowship as a whole. The Fellowship's definition of an OA group affirms this point: Any two or more compulsive overeaters who come together to practice the twelve steps and twelve traditions are considered a group, as long as that group has no other affiliations.

Groups which ignore one or more of the twelve traditions bring discord to the Fellowship. For example, groups have allowed disagreements to take precedence over sharing recovery in meetings. Other groups have continually depended on a handful of members for leadership, instead of trusting God to guide them through the informed group conscience. Some groups have limited their membership, ignoring the third tradition. Or, groups have accepted free rent, photocopying, and other services from persons and institutions outside OA despite our seventh tradition of being self-supporting. Groups have promoted non-OA-approved literature to their members, or focused meeting discussions on topics not related to recovery from compulsive overeating, forgetting our primary purpose as expressed in tradition five. Meeting time has been used to promote outside enterprises and issues, despite our sixth and tenth traditions. Groups and individuals have broken members' anonymity, even though two of our traditions deal with this important aspect of our Fellowship. In these and many other ways, groups sometimes fail to live by the principles embodied in our twelve traditions.

However, an infraction of an OA tradition does not result in a group being summarily ejected from the Fellowship—we might not have any OA Fellowship at all if that were the case!

When a group breaks one of the traditions, it's usually because members aren't well informed about them, not because members choose to ignore them. When this happens, OA members who know the traditions have a responsibility to speak up and to inform the group that it is operating outside the traditions. When they do speak up, a healthy discussion of the twelve traditions usually follows, and most groups elect to operate within these time-tested guidelines.

Even in cases where this doesn't happen immediately, the group soon finds out why every tradition is important. Our traditions exist to prevent problems. Groups which ignore traditions usually get into trouble of some sort. Problems arise, or, simply, the positive atmosphere in which the group has always operated changes. Members drop out, enthusiasm wanes, and the survival of the group is threatened. When this happens, members familiar with OA principles can pinpoint the source of the trouble as a broken tradition, and before long the informed group conscience moves to put the group back on track.

In extreme cases, where a group is affecting OA as a whole because of its persistent refusal to operate by OA principles, the group may be dropped from OA meeting lists which are published by intergroups and other OA service bodies. However, the service body taking such an action should do so only after much soul-searching. It is far too easy to use the power of the majority against groups in the minority simply because they have chosen a different approach to working the program, and not because they are truly harming other groups or OA as a whole by their actions. It is also easy for emotions and personality conflicts to enter into a decision not to list a certain OA meeting. When this happens, the tradition of autonomy is ignored and the unity of the Fellowship suffers.

In 1988, OA's Board of Trustees decided not to register with the World Service Office any OA group that placed special requirements on its members. At the same time, the Board allowed the registration of groups that placed specific abstinence or other requirements on officers or lead speakers, since these restrictions are not requirements for *membership* in the group. Still, the question arose whether or not this was a break of tradition four which clearly states, "OA groups should be autonomous . . ." In order to make sure group autonomy would be respected, it was left up to each group to judge whether the group's guidelines for attendance, sharing, or voting were suggestions or requirements.

Autonomy also means that OA groups operate free of outside influences. Even when other organizations provide us meeting places, we do not let them influence the OA group. Of course a meeting held in a church, office building, hospital, or school must conform to building rules concerning smoking, noise, tidiness, rent, parking, and the like. But non-OAs cannot limit members' rights to express themselves in meetings. Nor can membership be confined to members of the church, employees of the company, patients at the hospital, or residents of the area, since OA groups are open to all who have a desire to stop eating compulsively. Certainly outside organizations should not be allowed to interject their practices into OA meetings.

This was the case in OA's early days with a group which was hosted by a large church. Unfamiliar with the concept of OA autonomy, the group began to incorporate the church's practices into the OA meetings—laying on hands and praying for healing for those having difficulty with the program. Membership quickly soared to almost 300. Members of the group, convinced they had been forever healed of compulsive eating, forgot about working the steps. Soon they found themselves back in the throes of the disease. In a few months the group dwindled to a handful, and eventually it disbanded.

Our fledgling Fellowship learned a lot from this experience. We saw that OA autonomy is essential if we are to live by our traditions and keep OA's twelve-step recovery program intact.

As our Fellowship has matured, OA groups have found ways to meet their unique needs and still operate within the twelve traditions. Special-emphasis meetings are examples of this. In OA there are many meetings with a special emphasis, such as meetings for young people, for maintainers, for lesbians, for those who have lost a hundred pounds or more, or for those in relapse. Groups have the autonomy to follow formats geared to particular needs. Group membership is open to all compulsive overeaters, however, and all members should be given an opportunity to share and have a say in how the meeting operates. Within these guidelines, special-emphasis OA groups flourish and nurture the recovery of the individuals who belong to them.

The fourth tradition offers OA groups the freedom to find their own way and learn from their own experiences. At the same time, this tradition assures all of us that our OA Fellowship won't be harmed by the misguided actions of one group and that OA meetings will continue to focus on the principles embodied in OA's twelve steps and twelve traditions.

Living by the fourth tradition in OA means learning to act autonomously, even as we live in harmony with others. Here, we accept responsibility for ourselves, for our actions and their consequences, and for our own recovery. We learn to respect other OA members' autonomy when sponsoring or helping them. At the same time, we learn to accept other people's help without expecting them to do things for us that we should be doing for ourselves. We set necessary boundaries for ourselves and our OA groups so that we won't be abused by others, and we express our needs openly without insisting that others meet those needs in ways that might harm them.

How well do we live by the fourth tradition?

Does our group feel there are only a few right ways of doing things in OA? Do we respect the right of other groups to have practices different from ours?

Does our group always consider the welfare of all of OA in making group conscience decisions? In voting how to spend our group's money? In planning OA group activities? In the way we operate our meetings?

Do we stop to consider that our group's attitudes and actions will mold many newcomers' first impressions of OA as a whole?

Do we ever consider how our group's actions might affect the public's opinion about OA as a whole?

Does our group take time to discuss the traditions? Do we take all twelve traditions into consideration when making group conscience decisions?

Do we keep our group free of control or influence from outside of OA?

Do we practice the principle of autonomy by taking responsibility for our own actions and avoiding attempts to control the actions of others?

All of us need the balance implicit in the principle of autonomy to be the unique OA groups and individuals we were meant to be. Tradition four challenges us as individuals, as OA groups, and as a Fellowship to strike a healthy balance between our responsibility for ourselves and our responsibility to each other, while we grow together and work together as companions in recovery.

Each group has but one primary purpose—to carry its message to the compulsive overeater who still suffers.

We compulsive overeaters have been offered a wide variety of solutions to our problems, from diet clubs, fat farms, and counseling programs to powders, shots, and pills. In the midst of all this clamor for the overeater's attention and money, Overeaters Anonymous is unique in offering a spiritual program which has brought recovery to thousands who had lost hope. We who have found a sane way of eating and living have a responsibility to make sure OA doesn't become sidetracked. Our groups come together so we can share recovery through the twelve steps and the twelve traditions with fellow compulsive overeaters. OA will always offer recovery to those suffering from our disease as long as we remember that this is our primary purpose.

One important reason we stick to our primary purpose in OA meetings is so our groups can help us practice the twelfth step. Experience has shown we cannot keep the precious gifts of our own recovery unless we give recovery away by sharing OA's message. When we focus our discussions on the principles embodied in the twelve steps and twelve traditions, when we share how we've found the solution to our eating problems through practicing these principles, we discover that we carry the message to those who still suffer, and to ourselves as well. No matter how much recovery we have, we still need to hear the OA message. Every time we offer our experience, strength, and hope to the still-suffering compulsive eater, we give back what we have been given and thus continue the flow of healing power which fosters our own recovery.

Further, we OA members have the ability to help our fellow compulsive overeaters in ways that no normal eater can. We know this because we owe our own recovery to other OA members. Our doctors, families, or friends may have voiced their concerns about our eating problems or given us advice, but their words didn't seem to help. We felt they didn't understand us. In OA, however, we found people who had done and felt the same things we had. We began to listen eagerly to what they had to say. We wanted to know how they were getting well. From these experiences we discovered a key principle: The practicing compulsive overeater is more likely to find help from someone who has also experienced the pain of compulsive eating than from doctors, family, or friends. Speaking openly about our own struggles from the perspective of our OA recovery, we bring the suffering newcomer a message of strength and hope that is not available anywhere outside the OA Fellowship.

Tradition five reminds us that our recovery doesn't come from simply discussing our problems with each other. It is in the OA message—in our steps and traditions—that we find solutions to our problems. Living by these principles has saved our lives. Honesty, hope, faith, courage, integrity, willingness, humility, self-discipline, love, perseverance, spiritual awareness, service, unity, trust, open-mindedness, responsibility, acceptance, equality, and fellowship: These twelve-steps and twelve-traditions principles, rather than our problems, should be the focus of every OA meeting. The same thing applies when we sponsor other OA members. We help them most when we listen, avoid giving advice, and share our experience with living by OA principles.

An OA group is not a social club, though we make wonderful friends in OA and look forward to seeing them at meetings. Tradition five reminds us that OA groups often die out if group members form cliques or continually ignore the needs of newcomers, making no effort to welcome them or explain the basics of the OA recovery program to them. One OA wrote in *Lifeline* of her experience with tradition five:

"In my first years in OA, meeting leaders would suggest that we introduce ourselves to newcomers at break time. Despite their numerous reminders, I never did, nor did many other members. God only knows how many newcomers walked out of those OA doors, never to return. We must have appeared quite cliquish to them. . . .

"Things changed when my husband and I moved to a town where there were no OA meetings. My sponsor encouraged me to start one. I was scared, but I accepted the challenge. The group was small—only four of us—but we were eager to grow. We hoped for newcomers, but there weren't any. . . .

"Soon we learned that two of our four members would have to drop out because of scheduling conflicts. But before they left, we got our first newcomer! We fell all over her. At the break, *everybody* went up to talk to her. Suddenly I found that my fear of approaching a new person had vanished. My need for recovery far outweighed my fear.

"These days I no longer avoid talking to newcomers. I now approach them with open arms, thank them for coming, and encourage them to return. Without them, this group of ours wouldn't be celebrating its first anniversary!"[1]

The "compulsive overeater who still suffers" isn't always a newcomer to OA. He or she can also be an established member experiencing difficulties with the disease of compulsive eating or with other problems. Seeing one of our members go into relapse or face personal problems can be frightening to us, and we may react with condemnation toward the member who breaks his or her abstinence or has other kinds of difficulties. Often we're tempted to avoid the issue by avoiding the suffering person. Perhaps we use the slogan "stick with the winners" as a rationalization not to speak to the person in relapse at OA meetings, or never to call our friends who have stopped coming.

1. "Vital Connection," *Lifeline*, March 1990, pp. 20-21.

When we react in these ways, we're forgetting the primary purpose of our group, which is to carry OA's message of hope to those who still suffer—including those among us who have heard the message many times before.

Tradition five also tells us to look beyond our own group, to compulsive overeaters who have never yet attended a meeting. Our primary purpose includes a responsibility to reach out to these people in whatever ways we can. This is the reason each OA group spends a part of its funds supporting intergroups, regional groups, and World Service. These service bodies extend the hand and heart of OA into the world around us in ways that individual groups often cannot: by maintaining OA offices and phone answering services; by placing meeting notices and other information about OA in the news media; by staging special events, conventions, and marathons; by publishing meeting lists and literature about the program; by providing speakers and information for clubs, hospitals, schools, and other interested groups; and in many other ways.

Before OA many of us simply lived to eat. Now that we've joined together in OA groups, we have a new purpose. Are we making decisions which help us carry a message of hope and recovery to others?

Does our group concentrate sufficiently on OA's primary purpose? Do we focus our discussions on the twelve steps, the twelve traditions, the tools, and recovery from compulsive eating?

Do we welcome newcomers to our group and give them individual attention?

Do we try to make the OA Fellowship known to people outside who need help? In what ways do we support our intergroup, region, and World Service in their efforts to reach out?

Do we ever volunteer to help newcomers, out-of-town visitors, or other members in need get to our meetings?

What do we do to welcome back members who are returning to OA?

Do we make a point to welcome new members, talk with them, offer phone numbers?

Can new members find sponsors in our group?

Does anybody in our group make a point to call newcomers or members who have been missing from the meeting?

Do we remember that long-term OA members can also be compulsive overeaters who still suffer? How do we treat the long-term member who is facing difficulties with compulsive eating or with life?

For OA groups and OA individuals alike, the fifth tradition helps us keep it simple. We find that when we focus on our primary objective of service, we can begin to eliminate a host of unnecessary concerns. As we concentrate on carrying a message of hope to others, we are empowered to use our unique talents in ways that are truly useful to others. The result is better than any outcome we could have planned for ourselves, for we find a deep satisfaction in service as we join forces to share recovery in OA.

An OA group ought never endorse, finance, or lend the OA name to any related facility or outside enterprise, lest problems of money, property, and prestige divert us from our primary purpose.

Tradition five defines our primary purpose. Tradition six cautions each OA group to stick to the primary purpose exclusively, no matter how many outside enterprises may interest us as individuals.

The person answering the OA telephone or working in any intergroup office will hear all sorts of interesting proposals. People will want to come speak at meetings about beauty techniques or new cures for obesity. Members looking for work will want to post notices on OA office walls. Our Fellowship has been invited to affiliate itself with everything from health spas to footraces, from cookbooks to restaurants.

Misguided OA members have been known to use our telephone lists to solicit sales. Members who are unfamiliar with traditions five and six sometimes plug outside enterprises in OA meetings—everything from books and vitamin pills to treatment programs and church revivals.

Many of these enterprises are helpful and deserving of attention and support. Why, then, do OA groups traditionally make it their practice to say no to all such outside endeavors? The reason can be summarized in three words: *Keep it simple.* Though these enterprises may be worthwhile, they threaten to divert the attention of groups from OA's unique function, which is to carry the message of twelve-step recovery to compulsive overeaters who still suffer.

In the past, some OA groups have given away or sold a wide variety of non-OA-approved literature, pamphlets, and books published by outside enterprises. As OA has matured, however, more and more groups have decided to distribute only OA-approved literature at meetings. Whenever an OA meeting displays or sells non-OA-approved literature it implies that OA endorses the philosophy of whoever wrote that piece. OA-approved literature reflects the experience of many members of the Fellowship whose recovery is strongly rooted in the twelve steps and twelve traditions.

The sixth tradition helps OA groups fulfill our primary purpose of carrying the OA message. If meeting time is taken up with pitches for religious groups or other twelve-step programs, if newcomers can't tell the outside literature from the OA literature at our meetings, if members put their phone numbers on OA telephone lists only to be bothered by sales calls, the OA message of recovery soon gets lost. Those who suffer from the misery of compulsive eating need to hear about the solution found in working the twelve steps during our meetings and phone calls. They also need to know that there are no strings attached, no gimmicks, no stockholders demanding that money be made.

There are many treatment programs for people with eating disorders available outside OA. Most recognize the value of the twelve steps and take measures to involve their clients or patients in OA meetings. Although outside enterprises may endorse OA, OA does not endorse any of those outside enterprises. We welcome all who come to our meetings with a desire to stop eating compulsively, no matter what other forms of treatment they might be involved in as individuals. OA has no affiliation with any form of treatment or therapy.

OA groups often meet in facilities belonging to an outside enterprise, such as a church, hospital, government agency, or company. This implies no affiliation with the entity which owns the building where the group meets. OA groups traditionally pay rent for the use of meeting space in buildings owned by outside enterprises.

In one city, a local hospital opened an eating disorders unit, began bringing its patients to OA meetings on a regular basis, and then convinced one OA group to move its meeting place into the hospital's conference room. Many former patients of the unit soon became staunch OA members, and often speakers at the OA meetings by way of sharing their stories would mention the hospital program by name. Soon speakers, some not long out of treatment and not yet familiar with the traditions, were making pitches for the hospital program in the OA meeting. This began to happen so frequently that newcomers were given the impression OA endorsed this other program. At this point an OA veteran objected, pointing out OA's sixth tradition of not endorsing outside enterprises. A heated group conscience discussion took place.

"How can you be so ungrateful to the hospital after all the support they've given OA?" asked one patient. "Besides, my treatment there brought me to OA. I'm sharing my personal experience."

The matter was resolved happily with a simple suggestion. OA members need to be free to share their experience, but the group now asks its speakers to refrain from stressing the names of any specific outside enterprises, including the hospital's eating disorders treatment program.

In the years since our Fellowship began, many other related facilities and enterprises have sprung up to help the suffering compulsive eater. In addition to eating disorders treatment programs, there are clubhouses where we can meet and socialize, halfway houses, bookstores full of recovery literature for compulsive eaters, twelve-step ministries, counselors, retreats, and therapy groups. One crucial difference between these and OA groups is that, while many of them are based on the twelve steps, they don't govern themselves according to the twelve traditions. For instance, they may have professionals in positions of authority, they may have requirements for participation beyond a desire to stop eating compulsively, or they may have the profit motive as a primary purpose.

Many of these programs have been helpful to OA members, and we're grateful that as individuals we have so many choices to assist us in our recovery and spiritual growth. Certainly, we need feel no shame if we decide to supplement our personal recovery in OA with other kinds of support. Still, following tradition six, OA groups do not affiliate themselves with any such non-OA enterprises. We take whatever measures we can to make sure they don't use the OA name, and we avoid utilizing OA meeting time and space to promote them.

Nor is OA affiliated with other twelve-step-and-twelve-tradition groups, such as Alcoholics Anonymous, Al-Anon, or O-Anon, although many of us are also members of these. OA has often made use of the wisdom and experience of other twelve-step groups in making decisions for our Fellowship, but we are not a part of any of them, nor they of us. We have our own unique purpose to fulfill—providing a twelve-step-and-twelve-tradition Fellowship for compulsive overeaters.

As discussed in relation to tradition five, OA meetings focus on recovery from compulsive overeating. Members who put too much emphasis on other fellowships in OA meetings leave compulsive eaters with the impression that these programs and the problems they address are more serious or more important to the compulsive overeater, than OA. Such is not the case, and keeping the sixth tradition means that we refrain from pitching for other programs in OA meetings.

OA's lack of attachment to any kind of outside enterprise gives our Fellowship a marvelous freedom. We operate with a minimum of worry about funding, administrative problems, or the success and failure of non-OA ventures. By steering clear of any such affiliations, OA groups can concentrate on recovery from compulsive eating instead of on problems associated with money, property, and prestige which cause so much conflict in the world around us.

How do we respect OA's sixth tradition?

Does our group discourage members from plugging outside enterprises in OA meetings? Or do we rationalize that people need to hear about the program being discussed, so it won't hurt if we ignore the traditions this time?

When we vote on how to use group funds and other resources, are we careful to avoid financing outside enterprises?

Does our group sell or distribute outside literature at our meetings?

Are we careful never to use our OA group contacts for personal financial gain? Do we speak up when we see somebody else misusing OA phone lists and/or meetings in such a way?

When we share in meetings are we careful not to imply an OA endorsement of outside enterprises, such as hospitals, eating disorders treatment programs, other twelve-step groups, clubs, books, publications, ministries, and therapies? Do we overemphasize these and underemphasize our OA experience?

When we find ourselves or our OA groups embroiled in problems of money, property, and prestige, we have a clue that we might have involved ourselves in matters which would be better left alone. We cause these kinds of problems when we take on outside responsibilities or promote outside causes, diverting our group's attention and resources from OA's primary purpose of carrying the OA message.

"First things first" is another slogan which sums up tradition six. In OA we learn to focus on our primary purpose and exclude from our groups everything which might interfere with our ability to carry the OA message.

*Every OA group ought to be
fully self-supporting, declining
outside contributions.*

Tradition seven follows naturally from traditions five and six. If the Overeaters Anonymous Fellowship is to fulfill our primary purpose and remain free of outside influences, we must stay free of the need for outside contributions as well. OA ought to be fully self-supporting.

Certainly money is needed to keep the OA program alive. Each group has expenses such as rent or literature. When individual groups join to form an intergroup, opportunities to carry the OA message multiply, but so do expenses. Most intergroups provide meeting lists, have telephone lines or answering services, distribute information about the OA program in their communities, publish newsletters, and organize marathons and conventions. Many intergroups support local OA offices where the phone is answered, OA literature is sold, and twelfth-step work is carried out.

The OA regional service bodies stage conventions, publish newsletters, help new groups and intergroups get established, and carry the message in many other ways throughout their regions. OA's World Service Office also provides services which play a vital part in each member's individual recovery. These include:

publishing OA books, pamphlets, and *Lifeline,* our journal of recovery; maintaining worldwide meeting lists; and answering inquiries from all over the world about our program.

All of these efforts are paid for by *us,* OA members who make donations. Nobody is charged dues or fees at a regular OA meeting. We pass the "seventh-tradition" basket, and most of us are glad to contribute to keep our own groups and our Fellowship afloat. After all, OA is our life preserver, our means of recovery from the disease of compulsive eating.

Tradition seven tells us that the financial support of OA is our responsibility as members of the Fellowship. We don't ask for or accept support from outside sources. While OA is a worthy cause, ours is not a charitable organization. In fact, there is a limit on the amount that may be given by one member in one year to OA's World Service Office.

The reasons for this are clear. If we accept "free" gifts from outsiders, or too much from one member, we become less than free ourselves. We may become dependent upon the money being donated and never learn to take responsibility and pay our share. The need to maintain good relations with the donor diverts attention from our primary purpose. Meanwhile, the donor who is paying OA's way might naturally expect to have a voice in our decisions. The contributor of large amounts might well feel he or she has a right to dominate the group. This spells trouble, because our ultimate authority is a loving God as expressed in our group conscience.

Funds are necessary to keep meetings operating. In keeping with tradition seven we pay all group expenses out of the group basket, whether they be for rent, photocopying, coffee, or other supplies. However, we've learned by experience that it's not good for groups to keep large sums of money. When the treasury grows beyond a prudent reserve needed to meet short-term expenses, groups pass along these funds to their intergroups, regions, and the World Service Office. These service bodies require financial support if they are to continue carrying the message in ways groups cannot. Besides, excess funds inevitably cause problems for groups which accumulate them.

In one case, a group had been meeting harmoniously and growing rapidly for a year, but had never made an intergroup donation. Funds in the group treasury were well over the amount needed to pay the next few months' rent and the literature table was well stocked. Finally the group's treasurer brought up the subject of the excess funds. "We need more fun in our lives," she said. "Let's take that money and throw a party!"

Other members objected. "Mark, our group secretary, is moving out of town," one said. "We should buy him a nice going-away present with that money." Soon the group was embroiled in a dispute about how the excess funds should be spent.

Finally one member offered another thought. "I found out about this meeting when I called our intergroup phone line. Shouldn't we be sending the excess funds to intergroup to help pay for the phone and other services?" After a discussion of traditions five and seven, the group voted to keep enough of the money to cover expenses for the next three months, and to send the remainder on to help the intergroup, region, and World Service carry OA's message.

Another group, seeking to avoid accumulating excess funds, went to the other extreme and simply stopped passing the basket at meetings for a while. This solved the excess money problem, but kept the group from making needed contributions to its inter-group or other service committees. One week a member pointed this out to the group.

But a second member objected. "The seventh tradition says to be *self*-supporting. It doesn't say anything about supporting intergroup or any other service body."

"Aren't those groups working for *us?*" a third member asked. "They tell newcomers what OA is and how to find our meeting. If we don't do our share to support them financially, how can we claim to be fully self-supporting?"

During the next week, members of the group thought about the conventions and marathons, publications and meeting lists, and other help, information, and support which had been provided their group by OA service bodies. "Intergroup, region, and World Service are part of our group, too," they agreed. And they voted to keep passing the basket so they could contribute their share of the funds to keep these service bodies going.[1]

In cases where a group is struggling financially, the Fellowship as a whole might be glad to "carry" the fledgling meeting for a while. Over the long haul, however, this kind of dependency becomes unhealthy. As soon as possible, OA groups need to pay their share of the costs for the services they receive from other OA service bodies. The same principle applies to individuals in OA. Even those of us experiencing financial struggles find we need to make some contribution to our OA meetings. For many of us, our willingness to pay our own way is a sign that we are recovering and maturing emotionally.

The seventh tradition doesn't simply apply to financial support, however. In order to be fully self-supporting, groups and individuals need to take on their share of the service work as well. Financial contributions may pay for the intergroup's telephone line, for instance, but somebody in OA needs to answer the phone or return the calls. Money is needed to print and mail newsletters, but first, OA members have to write, edit, type, design, and address them. Groups need to send representatives to intergroup to help with the decision making, bring news back to the groups, and distribute the newsletters to meetings. Individuals must volunteer to help if OA is to host conventions

---

1. See *Self-supporting the 60/30/10 Way* (Overeaters Anonymous, Inc.) for information on how groups traditionally distribute contributions to intergroups, regions, and World Service.

and marathons. Our intergroups need chairpersons, secretaries, treasurers, regional representatives, and World Service Business Conference delegates. Meetings are fully self-supporting only when they contribute their share of the work that goes into carrying OA's message areawide, regionwide, and worldwide. Individuals are fully self-supporting only when they do what they can, when they can, giving back some of the help they have been given in OA.

Even as there is a limit to the amount of money the World Service Office will accept from any one member, there should also be healthy limits for giving service. When one member, or a small handful of members, continually does all the work, resentments usually arise. Other members sometimes feel excluded, so that OA breaks down into two groups—the "insiders" and the "outsiders." The insiders feel overwhelmed with service work and unappreciated. The outsiders resent the insiders for trying to control everything.

One OA group was started by a member who continued to do all the service work in the group for more than two years. She kept the key and unlocked the door, led the meetings, kept track of the funds, and represented the group at intergroup. She was puzzled, however, that her group never grew. In fact, it gradually dwindled until, finally, during the dog days of the group's second summer, everybody except the founder quit coming. As she sat there by herself for the third week in a row, she examined her service work in light of what she knew about OA's traditions. "I think H.P.

is trying to tell me something," she said to the empty chairs in front of her. "Maybe I need to let go of control here and let God take over this meeting."

The following week, another member showed up early for the meeting and asked if she could have the key. "I need to do more service work," she said. "Having the key will ensure that I get to the meeting."

The founder needed no further clues to her Higher Power's will. She got others to lead the meetings, and the group elected a new secretary, treasurer, and intergroup representative. Never again did she have to sit in the room by herself and wonder what had gone wrong with the group.

The principle of being fully self-supporting is an important one for OA groups and recovering compulsive eaters. In the OA group, we learn to depend upon God for our security, rather than upon other people. Under the guidance of our Higher Power, we learn to do the things we need to do to take care of ourselves and our group, materially and emotionally. We begin to look to our Higher Power rather than to other people as the source of our happiness and security.

Paradoxically, being fully self-supporting means we are now free to ask for help when we need help in doing OA service and in other matters as well. In light of the seventh tradition, we begin to see more clearly what our boundaries need to be. We begin to share our vulnerability with others in OA without expecting them to shoulder our responsibilities. As our Higher Power helps us to be self-supporting, we can let go of our unhealthy dependencies and develop healthy relationships with the people who share our lives.

How well do we practice OA's seventh tradition?

Do we really contribute all we can to OA's financial support, or do we just keep throwing a "buck in the basket"?

When the basket comes around do we keep in mind how much we might be spending if we were out bingeing, instead of coming to OA? Do we remember all the money we spent on weight-loss programs that didn't work?

Are those of us who are recovering financially willing to put a little more in the basket on behalf of the newcomer who can't afford to give as much?

Do we try to contribute something to the group basket, even when we're afraid of economic insecurity?

Does our group consider the group treasurer's job an important one and take care to make sure it is being done in a responsible manner? Do we listen carefully to the treasurer's report?

Does our group pay for its own expenses out of its meeting basket? Do we pay the going rate for rent at our meeting place? Do we pay for copying our phone lists, or do we expect somebody's employer to donate that?

When voting how to use group funds, do we keep in mind the things our intergroup, regional group, and World Service do to carry the message, and what that costs? Do we make a contribution?

Doing our share of the service work is also part of being fully self-supporting.

Does our group send a representative to each intergroup meeting?

Do we expect every member of our group to take a turn at doing OA service work?

Do we rotate jobs regularly, or do we have the same people doing the same services year after year?

Do some members take on more OA service jobs than they can effectively handle at one time? Or do we encourage less active members to become more involved?

The seventh tradition of saying no to outside donations and yes to our responsibilities as OA groups and individuals is a vital principle, keeping us and our Fellowship free of the complications that would inevitably arise were we to depend on outside sources. As long as we keep this tradition, paying our own way from our own pockets, we will earn the respect of the general public, and self-respect as well.

Overeaters Anonymous should remain forever nonprofessional, but our service centers may employ special workers.

OA is built upon a foundation of sharing our experience, strength, and hope, one member to another, with no strings attached. This principle of giving freely to one another makes our Fellowship unique among programs for compulsive overeaters. As OA members we may donate many hours of service to each other, sponsoring, speaking at meetings, and doing necessary committee and other service work. For this none of us receives payment in money. Our reward is something money can't buy—our own personal recovery.

The tradition of nonprofessionalism helps OA steer clear of the profit motive and concentrate on offering twelve-step recovery to all who seek it. Newcomers to OA are often impressed by the honesty they hear, the depth of sharing, and the spirit of compassion found at OA meetings. None of us is paid to be here. Each of us is a compulsive eater, and we all come seeking support for our own personal recovery. Knowing this, we can trust each other to speak from the heart, to share what our experience has taught us, and to listen compassionately to our fellow members.

Since there are no professional OA members, we all have an equal opportunity to share in doing service.

We don't need certification, education, or credentials to share our program with fellow compulsive overeaters or to take service positions at our home meetings. All we need is willingness and a commitment to the twelve steps and twelve traditions of OA. Each of us can play a key role. Since our twelfth step includes carrying the OA message, it's good that there are plenty of opportunities for all of us to be of service.

Professionals are hired from among our membership or from outside for their expertise or advice when such help is needed for services demanding special skills. Tradition eight says that "our service centers may employ special workers." Our experience has shown that some paid employees are necessary to take care of the business of OA in intergroup offices and our World Service Office.

For instance, in one city the intergroup decided to open an office. A nonprofessional volunteer was found to manage the office, making sure correspondence was attended to, bills were paid, the telephone was answered, supplies were ordered, and records were maintained. It was quite a job! After several months of faithful service, the volunteer manager got sick and had to resign. The intergroup began looking for a new volunteer manager. Two months went by, and the position was not filled. "I'd like to help out," people would say, "but I just don't have time to do that much service." Finally five OA members agreed to take care of parts of the task, staffing the office in shifts. This arrangement was better than no office management at all, but confusion was still the order of the day. Details continually fell through the cracks, and volunteers often had to let the office's business slide to take care of other priorities in their lives. Nobody, not even the landlord, knew who was in charge or whom to call when a problem arose. At last the intergroup accepted the fact that the office manager's job was too big to be handled by volunteers and too important to be left to chance.

"We can't afford it," they said, "but we're going to have to hire a manager."

So hire a manager they did. Although it wasn't a requirement that the manager be an OA member, they decided to look first among their membership, since a manager who was also in OA would need less training in order to answer inquiries about the Fellowship. A recovering member with the necessary business skills was found to manage the office for a reasonable fee, and OA in that city had its first-ever paid employee. Effective office management helped OA grow stronger there, and the growing membership was glad to pay the manager for a job well done.

However, we are never paid for the Fellowship service we give in OA—those hours we spend carrying the message of recovery to other compulsive overeaters. Members who lead OA-sponsored retreats or special events are reimbursed for their travel and lodging expenses, but are not paid for their leadership, even if they are professionals who command a fee in non-OA settings.

Some OA members have worked for hospitals and

eating disorders treatment centers as professional therapists and have found their OA experience to be of great value to them in this work. The question arises whether or not they are breaking the eighth tradition by accepting pay for working with eating disorder sufferers. Such people, however, are being paid for their work as professional therapists, not as professional OA members. To be sure, they may speak with their clients about their OA experience. But in the therapy groups they conduct professionally, they are in authority. They are responsible for applying their expertise in the field of psychology to the needs of their clients. When they attend OA meetings, they are simply OA members with no greater authority than any other member of the group, and they are free to focus on their own recovery. These "two-hatters" are requested to speak only about their personal recovery at OA functions to avoid implying endorsement of an outside enterprise by OA as a whole.

OA meetings are often very therapeutic, but they are not the same as therapy groups. One major difference between OA groups and therapy groups can be seen in the eighth tradition. OA has no professional therapists charged with responsibility for guiding and working with members of the group. Though most of us feel free to share our problems at OA meetings, providing psychotherapy is not the purpose of OA. During the recovery process, some of us have found we needed the help of a therapy group with professional leadership, in addition to OA. By working through some of our problems in therapy, we've been able to get our special needs met while we continue to focus on the twelve steps in our OA meetings.

The vast good which OA does for suffering compulsive overeaters worldwide is still, for the most part, done nonprofessionally by OA members who give back what they are so generously given. This spirit of no-strings-attached caring and sharing is one of the greatest strengths we have to offer as a Fellowship, for it carries with it a unique healing power.

In OA, we learn to give our loving support to others freely, without trying to advise people or change them; nor do we look to others to work our program for us. In keeping with our "nonprofessional" status in OA, we willingly share and listen to our fellow compulsive eaters, but we try to leave behind expectations that they should solve our problems for us, that we should solve theirs, or that others will repay us in some way for helping them. Service is its own reward. When we approach others in this way, we often find that they respond to us with a new depth of love and trust.

How well are we learning to live by the principle of nonprofessionalism in OA?

Do we sometimes try to "fix" other people in OA meetings by giving them our expert advice, or are we content to share our own experience, strength, and hope?

Do we try to speak as experts in OA meetings? On recovery? On medicine or nutrition? On sociology? On the Big Book? On the OA Fellowship or program? On psychology? On spiritual matters? Or even on humility?

When we're having trouble with the program, do we try to hide that from those we sponsor or from our OA group because we want to be looked up to as if we were "professionals"?

Do we set other OA members up as "gurus" or experts because of their experience or personal magnetism? Do we ever treat some of our members as professionals, forgetting that they come to OA for their own recovery?

Do we make other people responsible for our abstinence or other aspects of our recovery?

Can we distinguish what OA employees do from what members do in sharing their personal experience, strength, and hope?

Can we distinguish what therapists and workers in eating disorders treatment programs do from OA sharing?

When we keep OA's eighth tradition, we discover a beautiful spirit of caring service which becomes a powerful factor in our healing. We are all nonprofessionals in our support of each other's recovery from compulsive eating, giving and receiving support and fellowship with no expectations of return. Living by the spirit of this tradition, we can each turn to the one next to us and say truthfully from the heart, "I put my hand in yours because I care."

OA, as such, ought never be organized;
but we may create service boards or committees
directly responsible to those they serve.

Visitors to some freewheeling meetings of Overeaters Anonymous sometimes shake their heads and say, "Tradition nine is the tradition these people adhere to the closest. This group is never organized!"

Though our OA meetings may seem chaotic at times, chaos isn't the goal of tradition nine. What this tradition encourages us to do is remain as free as possible from the bureaucracy which tends to form around organizations, taking on a life of its own and obscuring the real purpose of the group. Everything we do in OA is geared to our primary purpose of carrying our message of recovery based on spiritual principles. Taking care of group business is very important. Still, as little meeting time as possible is spent electing leaders, voting on issues, organizing events, or making reports. Instead, we concentrate on sharing our experience, strength, and hope with each other, and on studying the steps and traditions.

In order to keep our meeting time as free as possible from organizational activities, OA groups create service boards, such as intergroups, to meet and conduct the business of coordinating local public-information activities, operating service offices, publishing newsletters, and planning special events. These service boards are organized. Intergroups have elected officers and bylaws by which they operate. Usually OA groups which have joined to form an intergroup will each send a representative to the intergroup meetings to help with business, get feedback on group problems, and report back to the groups what the intergroup is doing.

Though our service bodies need to be organized, OA as such is encouraged by tradition nine to keep the emphasis on fellowship, rather than organization. This tradition helps to ensure that God will always remain our ultimate authority in OA. Without an organized power structure in which to operate, no single person or group of persons can govern others. No rules can be laid down, no punishments handed out, no orders issued. To be sure, intergroups and World Service can drop from their meeting lists groups that continuously ignore our traditions, but no OA group can be fined or ordered to disband. OA groups don't operate under any charter from World Service or anyone else. On the contrary, World Service derives its authority from the thousands of OA groups all over the world.

Nor can any individual member be kicked out of OA. Members come and go at will contributing as much or as little as they see fit, and no power structure exists to require otherwise. Our experience has shown that no amount of organization will prevent chaos in OA unless we live by the spiritual principles embodied in the steps and traditions. Our personal and group survival depends upon adherence to these principles, not upon obedience to any power structure.

This tradition of "nonorganization" can be very disconcerting to those of us who long for perfect meetings that always operate smoothly according to rules everybody understands. Some of us feel insecure when we discover there are no rules, only suggestions and traditions, and no leaders with authority to enforce these traditions. After we've been around for a while, however, we begin to see that this kind of human-powered organization isn't necessary after all. Meetings which are far from perfect in our eyes can still offer us the miracle of recovery. Our groups make mistakes, but most manage to survive. In fact we find we can learn from these mistakes and grow stronger.

After observing this tradition in operation for a while, most of us begin to trust that there really is a Higher Power guiding the OA Fellowship through our group conscience. We can relax, trust God, and appreciate the wisdom of the ninth tradition.

Does this mean that when we see traditions being broken in our groups we should say nothing? Quite the opposite! When traditions are broken, individuals have a responsibility to speak up—lovingly and clearly—even when we may make ourselves unpopular with other members of the group by doing so. Often members break traditions because they don't understand them or the spiritual principles upon which the traditions are based. By speaking out when a tradition is broken, we help other OA members learn about these spiritual principles. It's one very important way in which we share our experience in OA.

Once we've spoken, however, we need to accept that conflict may result, that our words might not be heeded, and that we have no way of enforcing our understanding of the traditions within the group. We speak in favor of the traditions as best we can, leaving the results to our Higher Power.

One member wrote in *Lifeline* about how she spoke up for the traditions in a meeting: "Our leader for the meeting wanted to read to us from a little booklet by a religious leader. Before she began she said, 'I know this isn't Conference-approved literature, but does anyone object to my reading it to the group?'

"I quietly responded, 'You *know* I'm going to object. Our primary purpose during an OA meeting is to carry the OA message. We can do as we like outside meetings.'

"With that, the other members in the room urged her to do as she wished as she was the leader. A newcomer wondered why we shouldn't be allowed to share anything we thought might help. Several people were irritated by my objection and a comment was made about the need to be open-minded.

"The reading was awkwardly deleted and we proceeded with a less than serene meeting. Afterwards I was told that I'd made others feel it was too risky to volunteer to lead.

"As I experience the isolation and pain of standing up for my convictions, I am filled with questions. Was

I being a trusted servant willing to speak up for the traditions? If we resort to doing whatever we want to in a meeting, is it an Overeaters Anonymous meeting, or an Anything-Goes Anonymous meeting?"[1]

Most veteran OA members have found that standing up for our traditions is worth the risk that we'll be criticized or that meetings might be "less than serene." The alternative could be something worse for us than temporary unpopularity and conflict. It could be that if we were to sit by and say nothing while our traditions were ignored OA meetings would lose their focus on the principles of the twelve-step program. The great healing power we have found in these meeting rooms would no longer be here for us. Living by OA's ninth tradition means that we don't depend on some authority or power structure to enforce the traditions. We all take responsibility to speak out when they are being ignored.

In the same way, the ninth tradition doesn't mean that OA groups should never make guidelines for conduct at their meetings. When problems arise—problems having to do with such issues as meeting format, smoking, cross talk—groups often hold group conscience meetings to find solutions. Some groups hold these meetings apart from regular meeting time, so that they won't take up minutes needed for sharing; other groups hold group conscience discussions and votes during the regular meeting, so all the group's

1. "Since You Asked..." *Lifeline*, November 1990, p. 19.

members will be able to take part. Individuals who have a healthy respect for the group conscience will follow the guidelines the group has decided upon. As with our traditions, when the individuals are ignoring the group conscience, every member has the right and responsibility to speak out.

Once we have spoken our minds, however, the ninth tradition tells us to relax and let our Higher Power take charge of the meeting. We find we cannot force our will on the OA group, no matter how right it may seem to us.

How well do we practice tradition nine?

Does our group support our leaders and service committees? Are we critical of those who are giving service and suspicious of their motives?

Are we mature enough to take personal responsibility for the well-being of OA and for our own recovery? Or, do we expect "them" to take care of things for us?

Do we try to understand and support OA's service structure? Do we do our part in helping OA's different service bodies carry the message?

Do we use patience and humility in performing each OA job we take?

Are we aware of all those to whom we are responsible in any OA job?

Has our group made it a point to discuss the

twelve traditions and how they apply to us?

Are we afraid to speak up when we see traditions being ignored in our OA group?

Can we do the footwork in our OA service and trust the results to our Higher Power, even when things don't go the way we think they should?

Do we practice rotation of leaders in our group? Do we discuss how rotation of leadership relates to personal humility and the OA foundation of anonymity?

In Overeaters Anonymous, we have experienced how things work out for the best when organization is kept at a minimum. The order we once sought in rules and power structures we have found in freedom instead. Trusting our Higher Power rather than any organizational structure, we can now take responsibility for our shared lives and for the OA Fellowship in which we are recovering together.

Overeaters Anonymous has no opinion on outside issues; hence the OA name ought never be drawn into public controversy.

We live in a world which thrives on controversy. When we arrive at OA and first hear OA's tenth tradition, it comes as a surprise to many of us that this organization, so supportive of our recovery from compulsive eating, will not be moved to throw its moral weight behind other good causes. How can OA sit by and say nothing about the many social evils which seem to go unchecked in our world?

The reason is simple. Our members come from many areas and backgrounds, and we have many shades of opinion on every issue. If OA were to take a stand on one of these, we would immediately alienate some of our own membership as well as many of our fellow sufferers outside OA. By allowing controversy over outside issues to drive away people who need the recovery OA has to offer, we would take a step backward from our primary objective of carrying our message to the compulsive overeater who still suffers.

Does this mean that in order to maintain OA unity individual OA members must sacrifice personal freedom of thought and give up every outside concern and activity? Of course not. As individuals we are free to believe in and work for any cause we choose. The tenth tradition asks us to leave these issues outside when we walk through the OA doors. Even the most worthy of other causes has no place in an OA meeting.

The OA recovery program is essential to each one of us. Our very survival depends on it. Without it, many of us would soon be so thoroughly occupied with compulsive eating we would have little time or energy left to do anything else—including effectively supporting those other causes which mean so much to us. This is why we are careful to guard our Fellowship from even the slightest connection with outside issues.

Breaks of the tenth tradition often seem quite innocent, but they can have far-reaching consequences. This was the case when a newspaper columnist, syndicated around the world, stated in her advice column that a belief in Jesus Christ was an aspect of the OA program. Of course, OA has no opinion on Christianity or any other religion, but the general public doesn't know this. Even after clarification from the World Service Office regarding this misrepresentation, the same perception was again carried in a subsequent column. The reason, according to a member of the columnist's staff, was that, despite our official disclaimers, the columnist had received letters over the years from compulsive overeaters who had been encouraged at OA meetings to "put their faith in Jesus Christ." Many suffering compulsive overeaters of other religions and nonreligious individuals were no doubt needlessly discouraged from seeking OA's help because some members brought outside issues into OA meetings.

Having no opinion on outside issues also means that we don't oppose any such causes. Ridicule and disrespectful comments about religions, diet clubs, political beliefs, and other matters have absolutely no place in OA meetings. We don't need to belittle others in order to carry the message of recovery OA has to offer. In fact, negative talk and laughter at the expense of others usually interferes with the positive atmosphere of the OA meeting. Many of us suffer from the habit of negative thinking and speaking. We desperately need a positive atmosphere in our OA group if we are to recover. Thus, we see the wisdom of keeping silent about outside issues in OA meetings.

What, exactly, are outside issues? This question has arisen more than once among us. For instance, many OA members are also members of AA, Al-Anon, O-Anon, and other fellowships, and these groups sometimes have a place in stories shared in OA meetings. OA as a whole, however, has no opinion on any group or treatment for alcoholism, drug use, codependency, or other compulsive disorders, and we find it best not to get sidetracked by them in OA meetings. OA is unique in offering recovery through the twelve steps and twelve traditions to those who suffer from compulsive eating. This is a vital role that no other fellowship can fill. Thus, OA groups focus their discussions on recovery from compulsive eating, rather than on these other issues.

But what about other programs for weight loss and eating disorders treatment? These, too, are matters about which OA has no opinion. As individuals we might share our experiences with them, but as an organization, we have nothing whatever to say either for or against any of them. We speak for the OA program in our OA meetings and literature. Our experience with it, honestly shared, never fails to offer hope and strength to the suffering compulsive overeater.

Nutrition is an issue with which compulsive overeaters deal every day, and it may seem logical that this Fellowship should have as part of its program some very specific instructions on how each of us should be eating. Yet we do not. Instead, we work the twelve steps in order to meet our common goal, which is to abstain from eating compulsively, one day at a time.

In the early years, OA published suggested food plans for our membership. The "Grey Sheet" plan, the "Orange Sheet" plan, or the "Basic Four" plan was considered an essential part of the OA program to some. Others members, however, claimed that one or the other of these was not nutritionally sound. Finally, OA's trustees hired a panel of nutrition experts to pass judgment on them. As it turned out, none of the experts could agree on the subject of nutrition, and each quarreled with different aspects of our food plans. As a result, OA stopped publishing the plans. The group conscience of our Fellowship has since agreed that nutrition is an issue outside the scope of OA's twelve-step program. Today, the individual member is free to follow any food plan or not to follow one.

OA as a whole has no opinion on diets, food plans, food allergies, essential nutrients, or related matters.

In keeping with tradition ten, most OA groups will sell only OA-approved literature at their meetings, and do not use outside literature as a basis for their group studies.[1] Many books and pamphlets have been written which are worthwhile and have aided individuals' recovery but have not been approved by OA as a whole. A policy of not selling or using these books in OA groups certainly isn't intended to ban their use among our membership. It simply means we have no opinion whatever on them. OA's experience can be found in our own literature. Our books and pamphlets are products of the group conscience of OA as a whole and were developed, edited, and reviewed by committees made up of OA members from around the world. They have been approved by our World Service Business Conference as having broad application to our membership. This doesn't mean, of course, that we all agree with everything in them. It simply means that they focus exclusively on OA principles and the OA message of recovery from compulsive overeating through the twelve steps.

1. For many years, Alcoholics Anonymous books were the only books about the steps and traditions available, so they have been used extensively in OA groups. The Big Book *Alcoholics Anonymous, The Twelve Steps and Twelve Traditions of Alcoholics Anonymous,* and several other AA books are on the *OA-approved Literature List* (Overeaters Anonymous, Inc.). Many OA groups stock these on their literature tables and read from them as a part of their meeting formats.

OA's tenth tradition of concentrating on our message and avoiding controversy is one from which we compulsive eaters can learn much. It is summed up in the saying "live and let live." We find we can live happier and more effective lives when we focus our attention on doing our Higher Power's will each day rather than on conflicts.

Are we practicing the principle of tradition ten?

Do we ever give the impression that there is an "OA opinion" on diets? On diet clubs? On diet doctors? On diet pills? On psychiatrists and therapists? On eating disorders treatment centers? On churches or religions? On nutrition? On food plans? On exercise? On vitamins? On sugar? On other twelve-step groups?

Do we ridicule any of these or show them disrespect?

Can we honestly share our own personal experience concerning them without mentioning names or giving the impression we are stating OA's opinion?

In its meeting format and group practices, is our group careful not to imply that OA has an opinion on any of these?

In sharing at our meetings, do we try to help newcomers understand the twelve-step program of OA better?

Do we find OA more interesting when there's a

spark of controversy in the group? Do we ever bring up outside issues just to get people stirred up?

Are we afraid to speak up in favor of the tenth tradition when we hear others linking OA to outside issues?

Do we ever use our close contact with OA friends to campaign for outside issues?

Can we continue to share OA Fellowship—and even close friendship—with people who don't share our opinions? Do we concentrate on our common bonds, rather than on our differences?

Tradition ten frees us to concentrate on recovery from compulsive eating without the conflicts which seem to rage in the world around us. Many of us have been drawn to the excitement of conflict. Of course, no group or person can live completely free of conflict, but in OA we learn we can live, and even thrive, with a minimum of strife.

OA has excitement enough to offer, as we see hopeless compulsive overeaters recover through the miracle of the twelve steps. This could not happen if we allowed outside issues to turn our Fellowship into a platform for debate. For this reason, the tenth tradition of having no opinion on outside issues is one of our most carefully guarded practices in OA.

Our public relations policy is based on attraction rather than promotion; we need always maintain personal anonymity at the level of press, radio, films, television, and other public media of communication.

In Overeaters Anonymous we have found hope at last, a way out of the bondage of food and compulsive eating. Filled with enthusiasm for the OA program, many of us want to tell everyone who might be eating compulsively about OA. Carrying the message, after all, is an important part of the steps and the primary purpose of the OA Fellowship. The eleventh tradition gives us some guidelines for carrying OA's message, guidelines all OA members need to be aware of as we begin to share our program with those outside OA.

The first suggestion is that we publicize OA to the public at large without promoting it. Thus, we use the public media of communication—radio, television, newspapers, billboards, telephone book ads, handbills on bulletin boards, films, displays at health fairs, et cetera—to provide factual information about our program. We want people to know what OA is and how to find our meetings. In that advertising, however, we do not promote OA with personal appeals, celebrity endorsements, or other such means of persuasion.

Use of the media in this nonprofessional way allows OA to attract to itself those who are ready to take advantage of what we have to offer. Few of us who are now part of this Fellowship tried OA immediately the first time we heard about it. We may have needed this recovery program then, but it took a while for some of us to decide to come and to be willing to work the steps. Until we were ready, nobody could have "sold" us this program. As it was with us, so it is with other people who may benefit from OA. We carry the message best when we share frankly what OA is and what our own experience has been, without trying to tell others that they need our brand of recovery. In respecting the eleventh tradition, we respect the right of others to choose OA for themselves.

This is the public relations policy for the OA Fellowship. We do everything we can to tell people what OA is, how it works, and where we meet. We don't publish "before and after" pictures of our members in the advertising media. We don't promise quick weight loss or guarantee results. We don't have celebrities going in front of the public to talk about their success with our program and to invite others to join up.

In fact the eleventh tradition states that all individuals maintain their personal anonymity when speaking of their OA participation in any public medium of communication. In keeping the eleventh tradition, those of us who write books or are interviewed for a newspaper story or a radio or TV broadcast have two options. We can avoid calling ourselves OA members (even if we say we're compulsive eaters). Then we are free to use our full names or have our faces appear. Here the emphasis is on the individual, and we are not connected publicly with the OA program. Our other option is to go ahead and identify ourselves as OA members. When we do this we make sure our faces are not shown and our last names are not used. When we are careful to respect the eleventh tradition in this way, the emphasis remains on OA, rather than on ourselves.

In dealing with the media, we sometimes make the mistake of assuming that interviewers and photographers already know about OA's tradition of anonymity. Many media professionals have only a superficial knowledge about OA. It's up to us to explain the eleventh tradition and ask them to help us protect our anonymity. When we ourselves write about our OA membership for the news media or in books, we do not use our full first and last names in our bylines.[1]

It is no accident that the word *Anonymous* is part of our name. Personal anonymity at the public level shows the world that we take this tradition seriously, and that others can join us and be assured their membership will be kept private.

Some of us have protested, "I have nothing to hide. TV is a visual medium, and newcomers will be attracted by my weight loss and my story. Besides, I don't care who knows I'm a member."

This may be true, but it ignores the fact that OA is a spiritual program. When one person assumes the role of an OA spokesperson, his or her action poses

---

1. For guidelines for dealing with the media, see the *Public Information Service Manual* (Overeaters Anonymous, Inc.).

problems of a spiritual nature for the individual and the OA Fellowship. It poses problems for individuals because we have nothing of lasting spiritual value to gain—and perhaps much to lose—by publicizing our OA recovery. When we ignore the eleventh tradition we set ourselves apart from other OA members in order to take the role of spokesperson. Being "stars" can be fun, but inevitably our star status isolates us. Then we have a hard time asking other OA members for help when we need it. Humility is one of the essential qualities we must develop in order to recover from compulsive eating. Maintaining our anonymity at the level of the public media is one way in which we practice humility. It's one way in which we let go of personal ambition in order to keep ourselves in fit spiritual condition.

Those who ignore our eleventh tradition cause damage to OA's spirit of fellowship which is essential to our healing. Such breaks of anonymity may bring the OA name before the public, but they inevitably cause jealousy among OA members and competition for publicity and financial rewards. At the same time, breaks of anonymity misrepresent the OA Fellowship to the public by placing personalities before principles. They imply that one member's personal recovery or relapse is linked to OA's "success" or "failure." The eleventh tradition helps ensure that we don't hurt the OA Fellowship in our misguided attempts to promote it.

OA's insistence on personal anonymity and our refusal to promote our program through celebrity endorsements or other techniques of persuasion make OA unique among programs for compulsive eaters. Through our OA experience we learn that we don't always need to be promoting ourselves and our views to other people. Once we might have feared we would not be appreciated or loved if we didn't make a point of telling others about our personal or professional accomplishments. Now we can let go of that fear and quietly do God's will, trusting that the respect and appreciation we really need will come to us once we stop grasping for them.

How do we practice the eleventh tradition?

How does our group make its meeting place and time known to compulsive eaters who might want to attend?

How does our group inform the public—or support our intergroup in informing the public— about the OA program?

Is our OA recovery attractive enough to draw other compulsive eaters to OA?

Do we talk about OA so fanatically, or so often, that we make it unattractive to the people in our lives?

Are we careful to keep members' faces and names out of the story when we discuss OA with reporters or write about it ourselves?

Does our group or intergroup provide information about our eleventh tradition to the news media in our area? Do we ask them to keep all members' anonymity in news stories about OA?

Are we willing to speak up for the eleventh tradition whenever we see it being ignored?

"Attraction rather than promotion" is good for us and essential for the OA Fellowship. Our individual recovery, as well as group unity and effectiveness, depends upon this unusual brand of public relations. The eleventh tradition is based on faith in our program and in that Power greater than ourselves which guides compulsive overeaters to our doors. All we have to do is let the facts about OA and its principles be known. We can depend upon our Higher Power and this miraculous program to attract those who can benefit by what OA has to offer. When we maintain our tradition of anonymity we ensure that Overeaters Anonymous will remain a spiritual Fellowship, supporting all of us in our recovery.[2]

2. For more information on the subject of anonymity, see OA's booklet, *Anonymity: The Meaning and Applications of Traditions Eleven and Twelve* (Overeaters Anonymous, Inc., 1983).

*Anonymity is the spiritual foundation
of all these traditions, ever reminding us
to place principles before personalities.*

Living by the twelve traditions of Overeaters Anonymous requires that we adopt attitudes which seem strange at first to many of us. For instance, we place the welfare of the OA group above our own desires. We give up our aspirations to govern our fellow members. We welcome to our meetings all people with a desire to stop eating compulsively, no matter what we think or feel about them. We give up our dependence on authorities and power structures, along with our ambitions to climb to the top of some imagined OA ladder. We cease all attempts to use OA to promote our favorite outside issues and enterprises. We pay our own way and quit expecting others to keep OA going without our help. We give up all aspirations to gain professional status as OA members. We give up all ambitions that we might someday be acclaimed publicly for our OA recovery or service.

Behind all these self-sacrificing attitudes is a single spiritual foundation, so important to our Fellowship it is part of our name: anonymity. Without a foundation, no house can stand. It is essential that all of us understand and respect anonymity if OA is to survive and we are to find recovery here.

Our experience with the many aspects of anonymity starts when we walk in the door as OA newcomers. At that point many of us don't want anyone to know we're coming to OA or how we really feel about ourselves. In OA we find a haven, a place to share our feelings and experiences with other human beings who also suffer from the disease of compulsive eating. When we all respect the anonymity of others, we can trust that nobody outside these rooms will know we're coming to OA unless we tell them ourselves. Because ours is a program of principles, not personalities, we expect that what we share here won't be gossiped about or judged, either inside or outside OA.

Yet anonymity means a great deal more to us than just not gossiping. The quality of our recovery ultimately depends upon understanding anonymity as a spiritual principle, and how it enables us to change.

Many of us come to OA carrying the excess baggage of a lot of shame and pride. We are ashamed that we've been unable to control our eating by ourselves, and yet we're too proud to admit that we need help with our eating and our lives. In order to recover, we're going to have to let go of shame and pride so we can actively reach out to others for help. As we practice anonymity, we begin this process of letting go.

To be anonymous in OA means to be one among many, to accept ourselves as no better or worse than our fellows. This acceptance places us in a state of humility. It makes us teachable. We find ourselves listening intently to people whose last names we don't know. They may be younger than we are, or less suc-cessful by material standards. They may come from entirely different backgrounds. We listen because we identify with them. We've learned that they just may say something that will be key to our recovery.

More often than not, we go on a first-name basis in OA meetings, not because we're embarrassed about our OA membership, but because last names simply aren't important to us here. OA members may be famous or obscure. We may have many accomplish-ments or few, a lot of money or little. As we practice our tradition of anonymity, we affirm a very important truth. In OA we're all on equal footing—reduced to helplessness by our compulsive eating and freed to recover by this miraculous program. Money, intelli-gence, and status made no difference in our becoming compulsive overeaters and they make no difference in our chances for recovery.

Anonymity is not the same thing as secrecy. As OA's pamphlet, *The Tools of Recovery*, says, "It is not a break of anonymity to use our full names within our group or OA service bodies."[1] Many of us have found that our OA service work is made easier when we fully identify ourselves, and it becomes easier for others to reach out to us when we need help. While we bend over backwards to avoid gossip, we need to remember "it is not a break of anonymity to enlist twelfth-step

1. *The Tools of Recovery* (Overeaters Anonymous, Inc., 1981, 1989).

help for group members in trouble, provided we are careful to refrain from discussing any specific personal information."[2] For example, we might enlist such help without breaking a person's anonymity by saying, "Have you talked to Mary lately? She could use a phone call."

We need to remember, too, that not all members immediately let go of the gossip habit when we enter the doors of OA, and there may be newcomers present who are unfamiliar with our traditions. Therefore, it may be best to share in a general way during OA meetings and save the more intimate details for our sponsors or other individuals we have learned to trust in OA. Those who have walked the twelve-step path before us know the sacred trust of receiving personal inventories and the importance of anonymity. Many of us find that the unconditional acceptance and trust that springs from the practice of anonymity opens us to one another in ways we have never experienced before.

When we keep the twelfth tradition, no one person or group of people is ever given special status in OA. Our leaders have no special honors; they're simply our trusted servants. When we applaud someone's weight loss or celebrate abstinence anniversaries in our meetings, it doesn't mean we are singling out these persons for glory. It means we are rejoicing in a fellow compulsive overeater's recovery. The OA member abstaining

2. Ibid.

from compulsive eating is no more important than the member in relapse. Newcomers and young people share equally with OA's "elders" in our meetings. Some members are called upon to speak in front of large OA groups, but this doesn't make them more important than anyone else in the Fellowship. After they share, they usually sit down with the crowd and listen to the next speaker. They want to learn all they can, and they never know whom their Higher Power might choose to teach them.

In OA we learn that our recovery comes to us through the principles of the program, not through personalities. We discover that we can learn from and work in harmony with people whose personalities we dislike, as long as we focus on OA principles. Many an OA has had the experience of hearing from the lips of fellow members whom we heartily disliked the words which saved us when we were floundering.

Many of us have also had the experience of setting certain members on pedestals, only to have them climb down or fall off. Sometimes we've tried to build our program around one person we admired, a sponsor or a speaker. The day inevitably came when that person failed us in some way, and our own recovery was threatened. It was then we learned the importance of placing principles before personalities. We have found through years of experience that the principles of OA are failure-proof. They are the solid bedrock upon which we can construct meaningful lives.

Over the years our Fellowship has learned how

important it is to emphasize these life-saving principles rather than personalities when planning conventions and other special events. In the past, intergroups have invited OA members who are well-known as book authors, speakers, or eating disorders experts to speak at special events. The intergroups "headlined" those names on flyers and in newsletters. In some cases, hundreds of suffering compulsive overeaters flocked to hear the "name" speaker. It was a short-term boon but, over the long haul, problems arose. Some of these speakers were more interested in self-promotion than in the principles of the program. Some took advantage of their star status to plug their own books and treatment programs. Some struggling members placed their trust in these individuals, rather than in the principles of the program. In one case, reports of personal abuses arose. Because intergroups sponsoring the events had used these well-known members as star attractions, they found it difficult to prevent such breaches of the traditions.

After years of such difficulties, OA delegates to the 1990 World Service Business Conference voted to suggest that "intergroups, regions, individual groups, or any other sponsoring service bodies refrain from publishing the names or titles of speakers/leaders at OA functions in all materials (flyers, newsletters, etc.)."[3]

---

3. *Final Report—Overeaters Anonymous World Service Business Conference* (Overeaters Anonymous, Inc., published annually).

Anonymity fosters humility and guards against reemergence of that blind self-will that leads to the compulsion to overeat. Prevented by our traditions from placing ourselves or others in a position of distinction within our Fellowship, we find it easier for each of us simply to be a part of the group. Being a part of the group is essential to recovery from our disease of isolation. It means supporting and being supported by our fellow OA members and sharing openly the joys and challenges of our lives. These are things we could never afford to do in any group where we were trying to make names for ourselves.

Thus, it is to promote our own recovery that we cultivate the attitude of humility implied in tradition twelve. As we continue to grow spiritually, we begin to lose our desire for prestige in OA and in other areas of our lives. It is satisfaction enough to be in recovery—fully functioning and contributing as human beings. And we know we can't take all the credit even for that. We share credit with our Higher Power and our fellow OA members who have supported us and taught us so much. We also accept responsibility for our actions, looking only at our own faults and taking no one's inventory but our own.

In what ways do we act to place principles before personalities?

Does our group always inform newcomers about the meaning and importance of anonymity in OA?

Are we careful not to throw OA members' names

around, even within the Fellowship?

Do we ever repeat anything personal we have heard at meetings or from other members?

Do we value all OA members equally, or do we treat some individuals as stars or "gurus"?

Does our group support and trust our group conscience, or do we let one, or several, strong personalities run things?

Do we speak up for OA principles, no matter who might be displeased?

Do we ever confuse OA principles with our personal opinions?

Are we ever tempted to look at OA "success" as a vehicle for personal stardom?

Do we use anonymity to foster OA's primary purpose, letting members' identities be known within the group so we can be called upon for twelfth-step work?

What is each individual's real importance in the OA Fellowship?

As we recover in OA, we come to feel that anonymity is one of our most precious possessions. Anonymity is the spiritual foundation of our transformed lives, as well as of OA's traditions. We are compulsive eaters, living in recovery, no longer in bondage to food. We know that support for our recovery will always be here for us, as long as we remember to place principles before personalities, respecting these vital twelve traditions which bind us together in the Fellowship of Overeaters Anonymous.

We of Overeaters Anonymous would like to express our deep gratitude to our great preceptor, Alcoholics Anonymous, without which our Fellowship and our program of recovery would not exist. The twelve steps and twelve traditions are reprinted and adapted with permission of Alcoholics Anonymous World Services, Inc. Permission to reprint and adapt the twelve steps and twelve traditions does not mean that AA has reviewed or approved the content of this publication, nor that AA agrees with the views expressed herein. AA is a program of recovery from alcoholism. Use of the twelve steps and twelve traditions in connection with programs and activities which are patterned after AA but which address other problems does not imply otherwise. Here are the twelve steps and twelve traditions of Alcoholics Anonymous in their original form:

The Twelve Steps of AA

1. We admitted we were powerless over alcohol—that our lives had become unmanageable.

2. Came to believe that a Power greater than ourselves could restore us to sanity.

3. Made a decision to turn our will and our lives over to the care of God *as we understood Him.*

4. Made a searching and fearless moral inventory of ourselves.

5. Admitted to God, to ourselves, and to another human being the exact nature of our wrongs.

6. Were entirely ready to have God remove all these defects of character.

7. Humbly asked Him to remove our shortcomings.

8. Made a list of all persons we had harmed, and became willing to make amends to them all.

9. Made direct amends to such people wherever possible, except when to do so would injure them or others.

10. Continued to take personal inventory and when we were wrong, promptly admitted it.

11. Sought through prayer and meditation to improve our conscious contact with God *as we understood Him*, praying only for knowledge of His will for us and the power to carry that out.

12. Having had a spiritual awakening as the result of these steps, we tried to carry this message to alcoholics and to practice these principles in all our affairs.

The Twelve Traditions of AA

1. Our common welfare should come first; personal recovery depends upon AA unity.

2. For our group purpose there is but one ultimate authority—a loving God as He may express Himself in our group conscience. Our leaders are but trusted servants; they do not govern.

3. The only requirement for AA membership is a desire to stop drinking.

4. Each group should be autonomous except in matters affecting other groups or AA as a whole.

5. Each group has but one primary purpose—to carry its message to the alcoholic who still suffers.

6. An AA group ought never endorse, finance or lend the AA name to any related facility or outside enterprise, lest problems of money, property and prestige divert us from our primary purpose.

7. Every AA group ought to be fully self-supporting, declining outside contributions.

8. Alcoholics Anonymous should remain forever nonprofessional, but our service centers may employ special workers.

9. AA, as such, ought never be organized; but we may create service boards or committees directly responsible to those they serve.

10. Alcoholics Anonymous has no opinion on outside issues; hence the AA name ought never be drawn into public controversy.

11. Our public relations policy is based on attraction rather than promotion; we need always maintain personal anonymity at the level of press, radio and films.

12. Anonymity is the spiritual foundation of all our traditions, ever reminding us to place principles before personalities.

THE TWELVE STEPS

1. We admitted we were powerless over food—that our lives had become unmanageable.
2. Came to believe that a Power greater than ourselves could restore us to sanity.
3. Made a decision to turn our will and our lives over to the care of God *as we understood Him.*
4. Made a searching and fearless moral inventory of ourselves.
5. Admitted to God, to ourselves, and to another human being the exact nature of our wrongs.
6. Were entirely ready to have God remove all these defects of character.
7. Humbly asked Him to remove our shortcomings.
8. Made a list of all persons we had harmed, and became willing to make amends to them all.
9. Made direct amends to such people wherever possible, except when to do so would injure them or others.
10. Continued to take personal inventory and when we were wrong, promptly admitted it.
11. Sought through prayer and meditation to improve our conscious contact with God *as we understood Him,* praying only for knowledge of His will for us and the power to carry that out.
12. Having had a spiritual awakening as the result of these steps, we tried to carry this message to compulsive overeaters and to practice these principles in all our affairs.

The Twelve Traditions

1. Our common welfare should come first; personal recovery depends upon OA unity.

2. For our group purpose there is but one ultimate authority—a loving God as He may express Himself in our group conscience. Our leaders are but trusted servants; they do not govern.

3. The only requirement for OA membership is a desire to stop eating compulsively.

4. Each group should be autonomous except in matters affecting other groups or OA as a whole.

5. Each group has but one primary purpose—to carry its message to the compulsive overeater who still suffers.

6. An OA group ought never endorse, finance, or lend the OA name to any related facility or outside enterprise, lest problems of money, property, and prestige divert us from our primary purpose.

7. Every OA group ought to be fully self-supporting, declining outside contributions.

8. Overeaters Anonymous should remain forever nonprofessional, but our service centers may employ special workers.

9. OA, as such, ought never be organized; but we may create service boards or committees directly responsible to those they serve.

10. Overeaters Anonymous has no opinion on outside issues; hence the OA name ought never be drawn into public controversy.

11. Our public relations policy is based on attraction rather than promotion; we need always maintain personal anonymity at the level of press, radio, films, television, and other public media of communication.

12. Anonymity is the spiritual foundation of all these traditions, ever reminding us to place principles before personalities.

Permission to use the Twelve Traditions of Alcoholics Anonymous for adaptation granted by AA World Services, Inc.

For more information on Overeaters Anonymous
or for a copy of OA's literature catalog, write to
the World Service Office, P.O. Box 44020,
Rio Rancho, NM 87174-4020

OA books offer guidance to compulsive overeaters on the path to recovery

Item	Qty.	Price	Discount (10% on multiples of 100)	Total Price
The Twelve Steps and Twelve Traditions of OA				
#990 Single copy		$9.99	N/A	
#991 Box of 25		$224.75	Included	
The Twelve-Step Workbook of OA				
#992 Single copy		$6.99	N/A	
#993 Box of 25		$157.25	Included	
The Twelve Steps of OA on cassette				
#693 Two-cassette set		$10.00		
Abstinence: Members of OA Share Their Experience, Strength, and Hope				
#994 Single copy		$6.99	N/A	
#995 Box of 25		$157.25	Included	
Overeaters Anonymous (Brown Book)				
#980 Single copy		$6.99	N/A	
#981 Box of 25		$157.25	Included	
Lifeline Sampler				
#982 Single copy		$7.99	N/A	
#983 Box of 25		$179.75	Included	
For Today				
#984 Single copy		$6.99	N/A	
#985 Box of 25		$157.25	Included	

Subtotal =

Shipping – 10% of subtotal ($1.50 minimum) +

Total enclosed =

Send to:

Name _____

Street _____

City _____ County _____ State ___

Zip _____ Phone No. (____)_____

Group No. (if applicable) _____

I enclose a ☐ check ☐ money order in U.S. funds made out to: OVEREATERS ANONYMOUS

Please charge my ☐ VISA ☐ MasterCard

Card No. _____

Exp. Date _____

Signature _____

Mail with your payment to:
OVEREATERS ANONYMOUS
P.O. Box 44020 • Rio Rancho, NM 87174-4020 • FAX (505) 891-4320 ST

Prices subject to change without notice.